H.G. WELLS:

Critic of Progress

Also by Jack Williamson . . .

Bright New Universe

The Cometeers

Darker than You Think

Dome Around America

Dragon's Island

Golden Blood

The Green Girl

The Humanoids

Lady in Danger

The Legion of Space

The Legion of Time

The Moon Children

The Pandora Effect

People Machines

The Reign of Wizardry

Seetee Ship

Seetee Shock

Trapped in Space

The Trial of Terra

with Miles J. Breuer . . .

The Girl from Mars

with James E. Gunn . . .

Star Bridge

with Frederik Pohl . . .

The Reefs of Space

Rogue Star

Starchild

Undersea City

Undersea Fleet

Undersea Quest

H. G. Wells:

Critic of Progress

by JACK WILLIAMSON

Professor of English,
Eastern New Mexico University

THE MIRAGE PRESS

5111 Liberty Heights Ave., Baltimore, Md. 21207 U. S. A.

1973

Voyager Series V-107

Manufactured in the United States of America.

Library of Congress Number: 77-169989.

Contents

H. G. WELLS:

Critic of Progress

A Man Ahead

of His Century

1 The Future as History

The early science fiction stories of H. G. Wells are still great
fun to read—that's the first premise of this book. I fondly recall
the thrill of widened horizons they gave me in my own teens,
when I first found them reprinted on the stiff gray pulp pages of
Hugo Gernsback's then-new *Amazing Stories*.

The fat, red-bound volume of his short stories I bought at
college a few years later is still a treasure, for the way it brightened a rather desperate period of my life. Handicapped with
poverty and rawness, I was struggling to learn to survive and
create, much as Wells once had done. I used those wonderful
stories as a sort of mental tonic—as well as inspiring models for
the fiction I wanted to write—savoring each one for its liberation
of mind and its sturdy good humor and its brilliance of invention,
and I remember feeling a bit sad when the newness of each one
was used up.

Today, Wells is still exciting. Beneath all the fun, he displays
a remarkable mind—that's the second assumption of this book. He
is never a systematic thinker. Uncritical of his own ideas, he is
their captive more often than their master. Yet the casual insights
that illuminate his early fiction seem truer to me now than most
systems of philosophy.

I never saw Wells, but he must have been a delightful companion. Friends have praised the wit and imagination of his casual talk, his invention bubbling like champagne. Turning back to his early essay, "The Rediscovery of the Unique,"[1] and his later version of the same statement, "Skepticism of the Instrument,"[2] I am struck once more by the sheer quality of his brain.

In these brilliant essays, he is criticizing language and logic and philosophy. He sees the world as modern science sees it, an ordered flux of unique events. Aware that words fit things only obliquely, he understands the principle of uncertainty ahead of Heisenberg and the formulations of general semantics ahead of Korzybski. He perceives our limits. "The forceps of our minds are clumsy forceps, and crush the truth a little in taking hold of it."

The star student of Thomas Henry Huxley, Wells learned the scientific method, learned biology and ecology, learned to regard mankind not as the spoiled darling of God but as only another endangered species, threatened by the evolution of its own brain—which, to Wells, is simply an organic adaptation for survival, no sacred instrument of truth.

Wells wrote as easily as he spoke, sometimes tossing off his short stories at the rate of two or three a week. Science fiction brought him nearly instant fame when he learned to write it, and money to fill an aching need. Nearly all his great short stories and the novels of wonder that he called "scientific romances" were spun off in only half a dozen years, 1895 to 1901. They formed the foundation for all his later career, as social critic and utopian prophet and would-be schoolmaster of the human race. His art reached a peak in them, equalled only by the great comic novels of his next period.

Engagingly told and full of surprise, these early tales still shine with something more than Wells' wit and youth and appetite for life—with something new to fiction. They're timeless, because they put things to come in a fresh perspective. Wells, I think, was the man who discovered the future.

Men before him of course had always been awaiting their own tomorrows with uneasy hope or dread, and the seers and shamans and soothsayers had always followed their hazardous calling. A few such prophetic thinkers as Malthus had turned before him from magic to logic as a guide. But it was Wells, to quote his own *Experiment in Autobiography*, who made "the first attempt to forecast the human future and to estimate the relative power of that and that great system of influence."[3]

Futurology has lately become a recognized trade, complete with professional organizations and glossy publications, its findings as vital to modern commerce and war as those of astrology once were to barbarian emperors. But Wells seems to have been the pioneer.

His impulse toward the future must have sprung from his childhood resentment against the suffocating oppressions of class and poverty. The notion of rebellion may have been planted by his father, an open-minded easy-going man who never welcomed the mother's meek conformity.

His method of discovery applied the science of organic evolution he learned from Darwin's champion, old Thomas Henry Huxley. Other men were using it to illuminate the human past. Wells turned it into the future—his first great novel, *The Time Machine*, inverts the evolutionary process to project the long decline of life upon a dying earth.

Wells' first formal prediction may have been the essay he read to his college debating society in 1885, the year after he became Huxley's student. His ambitious title was "The Past and Future of the Human Race." There is more future-probing in the drafts of *The Time Machine*, begun in 1888. The earlier versions show Wells shaking off Victorian tradition and convention, show him learning to think at the same time he was learning his literary art, show him coming to view the past and future evolution of the human species with scientific insight and objective detachment.

In *Experiment*, he tells how the problems of the future came to dominate his conscious life. "I think my contact with evolutionary speculation at my most receptive age played a large part in the matter." As he sharpened his focus on the future in finishing *The Time Machine* and working out such later stories as *When The Sleeper Wakes*, it struck him that "there might be better guessing about the trend of things."

Attempting that better guessing, he greeted the new century with *Anticipations*, which he says was not only a new start for him but also "a new thing in general thought." He calls it "a comprehensive attempt to state and weigh and worked out a general resultant for the chief forces of social change throughout the world, sober forecasting, that it is to say, without propaganda, satire, or extravagance." He documented and defended his achievement in another book, *The Discovery of the Future*, published in 1902.

These two books are the charter documents of futurology. Here Wells establishes a basis for the discipline, outlines its methods, and attempts the first forecasts—in some details strikingly right, in others just as strikingly wrong. For all the fumbling, he has hit on a new thing. As he puts it, he is writing the human prospectus.

The view of the future announced in these two books at the dawn of this century can give us a new perspective on Wells' whole career. It explains not only the brilliance of his early science fiction but also his later turn from literature to education and pamphleteering.

Looking first at the science fiction, we find that he was not simply fictionizing his visions of times to come. Though he sometimes did that, the full truth is more complex. His rationale for factual prediction seems to have evolved from his technique for creating fantasy.

The method of his fiction is to mix recognition and surprise. With the observant care of a chemist testing some unknown compound against familiar reagents, Wells introduces selected novel elements into familiar situations. The essentials are first to limit each story to one new premise, and then to develop the consequences in a strictly logical way.

Writing fiction, Wells applied this method impartially to possible and impossible premises, to visiting angels and invading Martians, to makers of diamonds and workers of miracles. The results are explored more fully below. Here we need only note that he has worked out the basic technique of futurology.

Future events, after all, are not simply possible or impossible. They are only more or less probable. Though Jules Verne could never understand or forgive Wells' willingness to accept the fantastic premise, it extends the power of his method in a very significant way. In projecting factual futures, he can follow any selected factor to the vanishing point of likelihood.

He is simply applying the method of experimental science, using his trained imagination for a laboratory. Some single selected factor is varied at will, while everything else is controlled. In a story, that variable may be the premise that magic works—but only within a limiting frame of stated conditions. In futurology, held within the same sort of controlled rational frame, the variable may be any technological or cultural premise that needs examination.

Today's futurologists have elaborated the procedures. They draw more data from more disciplines. They process it in computers. They talk of Delphology, of model-building, of scenarios. But their operating principles have not gone far beyond those Wells laid down in those two early books.

A quarter-century after Wells' death, the definitive life and letters is still to appear. However regrettable, this long delay is not hard to understand. Critics have always been bewildered by the bulk and variety of his writing, and have generally tended to ignore or belittle the masses of material that failed to fit their preconceptions. His discovery of the future might serve as a useful key to his whole career.

Seen through his sense of the future, the contradictions begin to melt away. He dismayed and hurt his friends when he gave up his literary art to turn social reformer, because they failed to grasp his suggestion that the conditions of the future "could be brought within our knowledge and its form controlled." The notion of control had seized his mind. His method had not revealed any one determined destiny for the human race, but rather allowed him to explore many alternative futures, all more or less probable, most of them disturbing. He set out to avert the worst of them.

Still filled with the vigor of youth, his cockney self-confidence not yet dimmed, he tried to engineer a better world than any he expected. Most of the rest of his life was devoted to that mission, and most of what he wrote can be related to it.

This invention of futurology is a decisive turning point in Wells' career. Most of his early science fiction, done while he was still finding and testing his discovery techniques, is darkly pessimistic about our human destiny. Through the middle years of his life, hopeful of knowing and reshaping our common fate, he is often optimistic. As the years and wars go by, as his most frightening predictions loom closer in spite of all his toil, he is often disheartened and embittered. But he keeps on campaigning to the very end.

The shift in Wells' thought around the turn of the century is so great that by 1905, the author of A Modern Utopia seems almost a different man. It is this later Wells, the teacher and reformer and prophet of science, who soon became the target of the anti-utopian satirist. Mark Hellegas has pointed out the odd fact that these more recent critics of progress have used the methods and often even the images of the early Wells to attack his later efforts to aid the evolution of a better world society.

What changed Wells, I believe, is the shift in his whole mental perspective that followed the discovery of the future. The earlier Wells had been a child of the past, a conscious disciple of Jonathan Swift, writing The Time Machine and The Island of Dr. Moreau and The First Men in the Moon almost as additional voyages of Gulliver. The later Wells, in his moments of hope, sees no limits.

At the end of the early versions of his *Outline of History*, written to educate mankind for citizenship in the better world he hopes to build, he prophesies that the victory for global unity and peace will lead only "to new and vaster efforts," until human life, in one of his favorite images, "will presently stand upon this earth as upon a footstool, and stretch out its realm amidst the stars."

Though others before him had peered into the future, most of them tried too soon. The essential silent assumption of futurology is the notion of systematic change, observed in the past and projected upon possible tomorrows. Wells, learning ecology and biology and the fact of organic evolution from Darwin's great disciple, was among the first to see their use as lenses into time. He himself was sure he had found something new, as he testifies in *Experiment*, and certainly no rival futurologist has ever been so widely known or so close to controlling the shape of things to come as he seemed to be at the summit of his career.

2 Wells and Modern Science Fiction

This book is a study of the great science fiction that Wells produced in the early years, before his discovery of the future was quite complete. We can only glance at his later utopian hopes, at his world acclaim, at his final bitterness.

Here he is still the second Swift, sadly aware of the animal heritage and all the hostile forces that oppose our dreams of progress. Here, I think, we have his most enduring monument, certain to survive all his later efforts to train and warn and coax the human race into his new social order.

These stories create modern science fiction. The yearly awards for achievement in the field, the "academy awards" of science fiction, are called Hugos, in honor of Hugo Gernsback, who founded the first science fiction magazines. With greater justice, they might be Herberts, in recognition of Herbert George Wells.

Gernsback did serve science fiction, by coining the term, by launching magazines, by zealous promotion, by writing science-packed fiction of his own. One of the magazines he founded was *Amazing Stories*, the first all-science fiction magazine. His greatest service, perhaps, was the rediscovery of H. G. Wells for a new generation of readers.

The first issue of Gernsback's *Amazing Stories* (April, 1926) reprints Wells' "The New Accelerator"—a light-hearted parable of progress in which a biologist invents a drug that speeds up life to such a degree that the rest of the world stands motionless. He and the narrator play pranks on statue-like people too slow to see them, and find their own clothing scorched by friction with the air. They later perceive that the invention "like all potent preparations . . . will be liable to abuse." But the danger to society is not their concern. "We shall manufacture and sell the Accelerator, and, as for the consequences—we shall see."[3]

The second issue of *Amazing* carries "The Crystal Egg," described as "a tremendous story by one of the greatest living scientifiction writers." A magnificent cover by Frank R. Paul depicts the fantastic beings that Wells' pathetic little Mr. Cave observes on Mars.

For the next twenty-seven months, Gernsback continued to feature Wells in every issue, his name first among the two or three in large type on each cover. Nearly all the great early novels were reprinted in *Amazing—The Time Machine, The Island of Dr. Moreau, The Invisible Man, The War of the Worlds, The First Men in the Moon,* as well as most of the best short stories.

When Gernsback added *Amazing Stories Quarterly* to his chain in 1928, he featured the other great early novel, *When the Sleeper Wakes,* complete in the first issue, with another colorful Paul cover, announcing it as "one of the first greatest scientific stories that have been written so far."[4]

There's an odd anomaly here, in the fact that Gernsback built his first science fiction magazines so largely on the starkly pessimistic work of the early Wells, for Gernsback presented himself as the optimistic prophet of progress through popular science. Preaching the educational value of science fiction, he went so far as to list an impressive panel of "nationally known educators" employed to vet the factual content of the fiction in his later publication, *Science Wonder Stories.*

Wells was no such optimist, least of all when he wrote the stories Gernsback was reprinting. As this book tries to show, he was always doubtful of any ultimate goodness in reason or science, always darkly skeptical of any moral or human values resulting from progress.

Not that Wells uses these early stories to preach any gospel of doom. The sermons and lectures come later. Here he's still the literary artist, not yet at war with Henry James, but still wrestling to resolve the profound inner conflict we shall try to analyze. Out of the agony of that bitter inner struggle, he—and not Hugo Gernsback—created modern science fiction.

Of course he isn't the sole creator. The tale of the fantastic voyage is at least as old as Homer's *Odyssey*. Defoe had invented a technique for fusing fact and imagination. Poe and Verne and many others had mixed fact and fiction.

But Wells formed the *genre*. He invented its methods of projecting possible futures, defined and explained its narrative techniques, created many of its most-imitated examples. His tales are the first and often still the best of most of its popular types.

The notion of invasion from space, that enduring cornerstone of the horror-film industry and the source of Orson Welles' famous panic-making broadcast and the theme of such a recent bestseller as *The Andromeda Strain,* springs from Wells' unforgettable *War of the Worlds*.

The notion of travel in time, though exploited by Mark Twain and others, had belonged to the shadowland of fantasy until Wells brought it into science fiction with his carefully logical theory of a temporal dimension in which his traveller can reach the present or the past by riding something like a bicycle in a direction at right angles to the three familiar dimensions of space. Since then, the time-travel paradox had become a too-familiar staple of science fiction.

In "The Plattner Story" and "The Stolen Body" and *The Wonderful Visit,* he drew the blueprints for all the later tales of parallel universes. Gulliver's Brobdingnag had been pure fantasy; in *The Food of the Gods,* Wells makes giants possible. In "The Story of the Late Mr. Elvesham," he anticipates the ethical problems of organ transplants when his hero finds his mind exchanged into an old man's body.

Wells invented germ warfare in "The Stolen Bacillus," tank warfare in "The Land Ironclads," and air war in *When the Sleeper Wakes*. By 1913, in *The World Set Free*, he had invented uranium bombs, foreshadowing all the later literature of atomic holocaust.

His heroes fight giant ants, giant prehistoric birds, and monstrous raiders out of the sea. They work miracles, create men, dream of Armageddon, and walk invisible. If such wonders seem trite now, they were new enough eighty years ago, exciting enough to inspire countless retellings.

John W. Campbell, a better editor than Gernsback, owes his own debt to Wells, one most clearly seen in the policy he announced for *Unknown,* the fabulous magazine of fantasy he edited for thirty-nine issues, March 1939 to October 1943. To quote a letter to me:

"I want simple, clear, and direct writing. You can't convince a man of normal intelligence of something he knows darned well is cockeyed by any amount of argument. On the other hand, he'll accept any premise you want to set up for the sake of a story. Therefore, magic is acceptable, if you *say* it's magic, and simply say that magic works. Period. You can't convince him it does, but he'll go along with you for the fun of it."

This policy statement for *Unknown* is a good description of Wells' practice in the early fiction. It almost paraphrases the prescription for fantasy that Wells himself set down. Calling his novels "scientific romances" to distinguish them from the "anticipatory inventions" of Jules Verne, he says in a preface that such fantasies "have to hold the reader to the end by art and illusion and not by proof and argument." A far cry, this, from Gernsback's notion of fiction for the sake of educational science. Wells' own narrative strategy for fantasy, as we have seen, requires just one carefully limited new premise or assumption in each story, following which "the whole business of the fantasy writer is to keep everything else human and real."[5] As he says in *The Wonderful Visit,* "Explanations are the fallacy of a scientific age."[6]

Sometimes, as here, Wells seems to blur the line between fantasy and science fiction. Sometimes he serves a delightful mixture of both. In *The Wonderful Visit,* Heaven exists in a "perfectly possible" twin universe, out of which an angel falls into the everyday reality of Siddermorton Park. Yet the line does exist. However blurred, it is generally distinct enough to define Wells' early science fiction.

In most respects alike, science fiction and fantasy both project illusions. The illusions of good fantasy come from story and style, from all the stuff of poetry. So do those of good science fiction—but with a difference. To the arts of language, science fiction adds a special sense of potential reality. Although its wonders are not yet, they aren't impossible either. Somewhere, sometime, they might come to pass. This element of prophecy is part of the spell of the early Wells. He creates an uneasy conviction that actual Martians might invade our unsuspecting earth, or he lights a spark of bright belief that a perfectly real machine might take us touring down through time to witness the end of the world.

This is not to claim that most science fiction is seriously

prophetic. The writer in search of a new idea is prone to choose the least likely future, not the most likely. As a story forms itself, the feeling of scientific possibility is often overshadowed by character and symbol and action. Perhaps no more than two percent of published science fiction is based on serious extrapolation from known science, but it is an influential and often-imitated two percent, and it includes much of Wells.

As a master of science fiction, Wells was absorbed with what I feel to be its most exciting theme: the impact of technology upon the future of mankind. The basic method of such "hard" or "straight" science fiction as his *When the Sleeper Wakes* is to project the not-yet-realized promises of science into an imagined setting where the human and cultural consequences can be explored. Doing this, the writer has to take a stand. Even the purest space opera, written and read for absolute escape, implies an attitude toward progress. Any imagined world must be in some way worse or better than our own.

The notion that man might use his mind to design a better world is at least as old as Plato's *Republic*—a book that once excited Wells. The pessimistic ridicule of man's misplaced faith in his own feeble reason dates at least from Aristophanes. But in our own technological age that ancient question has suddenly become too urgent to be left to philosophers. Our survival hinges on it, as Wells understood. That awareness made him the pioneer futurologist, the tireless crusader for the new world society in which he saw our only haven from self-contrived extinction.

As savior of humanity, at least in the short run, he must be ruled a failure. Our best efforts at world union, the League of Nations and the United Nations, have fallen fatally short of his bold design. Watching a world that seems poised forever on the brink of the fate he feared, it is easy to sense the despair that led the forsaken prophet, in the midst of World War II, to write *The Mind at the End of Its Tether*.

As science fiction writer, he was more successful. The *genre* is still what he made it. Most of a century after his early work, he still occupies a central place in the history of the form. A worthy disciple of Swift, he wrote such unforgettable satires as *The Island of Dr. Moreau* and *The First Men in the Moon*. In *The Future as Nightmare: H. G. Wells and the Anti-Utopians*,[7] Mark Hillegas has traced Wells' own legacy to a whole school of more recent pessimistic fiction—to Eugene Zamiatin's *We*, to Aldous Huxley's *Brave New World* and George Orwell's *1984*, to Kurt Vonnegut's *Player Piano*, to Pohl and Kornbluth's *Space Merchants*, to the too-perfect robots that I called the humanoids.

Wells' commanding stature in modern science fiction seems to be gaining recognition, even in the university. I have been surveying the multiplying college courses in this just-admitted subject. Compiling a reading list of the texts most frequently assigned, I was surprised as well as pleased to find three of Wells' novels among the first thirteen.[8]

Another cheering mark of this new academic regard is the symposium on "H. G. Wells and Modern Science Fiction" organized and lead by Darko Suvin in October, 1971, at McGill University, Montreal. Canadian Wellsians were joined by visitors from the United States, France, and Japan. Julius Kagarlitsky, author of a new Russian study, had also been invited but was unable to attend.

Wells' Darwinism was the topic of J. P. Vernier, author of *H. G. Wells et son temps* (Rouen, 1971), and others echoed the same biological theme. Suvin examined a retrograde evolutionary process as the structural frame for *The Time Machine*. My own paper, drawn from this book, showed Wells' debt to Darwin and Huxley for his discovery of the future. David Hughes explored his use of the garden as a Darwinian metaphor.

Kenneth Newell read an introductory essay. Richard Dale Mullen, in a study of "Wells in his Seventies," stressed the remarkable volume and vigor of his later work. Sakyo Komatsu discussed his recent rediscovery in Japan and his impact upon the new science fiction there. Robert Philmus traced his influence to Argentina in a contribution called "Wells, Borges, and the Labyrinths of Time."

This meeting did more than show a renewed regard for Wells as a creative artist and penetrating critic of his times and our own; it signalled a growing awareness of modern science fiction as his most significant and enduring creation.

3   Wells Against the World

An amateur in criticism, I feel bound to no particular school. Like the New Critics, I prefer to concentrate on the work itself. I want to read Wells' stories not as late Victorian cultural artifacts or as symbols for interpretation in the psychoanalysis of the author, but rather as creations worth study for their own form and value.

Yet no work of art exists in isolation. Wells' science fiction is the expression of a unique human being, responding during a crisis of his private life to a particular social environment. To understand the fiction, we must at least glance at the man and his times. As critics, we should neglect nothing that can illuminate the work.

Though Wells later announced that he was no artist, this early fiction was done with genius and care—we can trace *The Time Machine* through seven evolving revisions. The stories are, I think, satisfying aesthetic forms. They also reflect Wells and his world. They reveal the boldness and the pain of his responses to his mother's submissive piety, to his father's evasive independence, to all the barriers of faith and class and wealth he found in his way.

At a deeper level, I believe, the idea of progress served Wells as a sort of symbol for a conflict both more intimate and more universal. Challenging the hope of progress, he was perhaps unconsciously expressing the inevitable resistance of social tradition to all the impulses of the individual ego. I plan to document this idea throughout the book, but I think it needs an introduction here.

In a general sense, of course, the conflict requires no introduction. We have all endured it. From the moment we were born, society has been battering us with all her institutions. First of all the family, masking intolerable demands in cruelest tenderness. Then the school, the church, the law, the economic system, each forever crushing our private wishes and gnawing at our personal freedom. Born naked shrieking individuals, we have all reached some kind of truce with the world around us. Through lives of often painful compromise, we have bartered ourselves for love and bread and sheer survival.

As the stuff of literature, this eternal conflict is equally familiar. There are three basic patterns of plot: man against nature, man against society, and man against himself. Only the first, the most primitive story-type, allows the self to win—sometimes. In the second, the needs of the individual are commonly sacrificed to the claims of the race. The third is the pattern of classical tragedy, in which an overweening ego contrives its own destruction.

In the case of Wells, an ego of uncommon resource and vigor collided with social forces of uncommon strength. The unique outcome can never be fully explained. I think we can see the nature of the conflict and the shape of his solution a little more clearly, however, as consequences of a peculiar division in our

Western culture.

Every culture, as its most essential function, attempts to enforce its own solution to this perpetual rebellion of its individual members. In our own culture, however, the accidents of history have left us a choice that Wells was finally free to make.

We owe this choice, I think, to the contrast between the two chief roots of our civilization, the rigid theocracy of old Egypt, whose enduring symbol is the stone pyramid, and the loose tribal organization of the primitive Indo-Europeans, whose lasting monument is our language.

In Egypt the self was nothing. Every individual from pharaoh to slave was molded to fit his narrow place in the overwhelming social structure. Even today, its old piles of life-crushing stone and the relics of its cruel gods are acutely depressing to me.

This self-annihilating pattern of social discipline has come down to us through those escaped Egyptian slaves, the Hebrews, whose jealous YHVH was originally not much more merciful than Set. The Egyptian human type reappears in the prophets of the Old Testament as they call down the wrath of deity to help them impose their stern social restrains upon egoistic kings.

Among the Indo-Europeans, the self stood for more. Odysseus is the type. An unfettered and highly competent individual, he enjoys an indomitable self-confidence and a wide-ranging freedom that even a pharaoh might envy. He's Athena's favorite, by no means her slave. Men of his pattern challenged Egypt, sacked Rome, built the myth of progress.

Wells grew up in the shadow of Egypt, manifest in his mother's apprehensive piety and the rigid orthodoxy of her whole servant class. His father may have been only a hamstrung Odysseus, but his unrestrained Uncle Williams was a more infectious Greek. In the library at Up Park, where his mother was housekeeper, he found Plato's *Republic*, which did more than any other book to release his mind.

Wells' science fiction can be read as a shifting metaphor, I think, for the saga of his own impulsive ego in revolt against the sanctions of Victorian society. His heart yearns for the freedom of the Greeks, symbolized in the heroic dream of man-directed progress. But he is haunted by the cold social voice of Egypt, warning him that men are not heroic, that their works can't reach perfection, that the self must be surrendered.

Outlined so baldly, the proposition falls somewhat short of the whole truth. The Hellenic and Hebraic elements in our culture are intricately fused, and neither was ever absolute. Odysseus himself was often frustrated, even by his own humane Homeric gods; his private freedom was a very relative thing. The abler Hebrews and Egyptians must just as often have earned entirely selfish satisfactions as the chosen spokesmen for their more fearful deities. Wells himself was an extremely complex human being, who filled his long life with bewildering contradictions.

Yet, taken with such reservations, the history of his long guerrilla resistance to the forces of society can illuminate his character and his work. His early fiction is alive with its tensions. In story after story, we find his restless ego personified in the shape of progress, at war with his whole environment, defeated at last by the symbols of society and the nature of the world.

4   About this Book

The first version of this book was written in 1962 and 1963 as my dissertation for the doctorate at the University of Colorado. I had been allowed to do a master's thesis on contemporary science fiction,[10] and my first proposal was a general study of Wells' early fiction. When Bernard Bergonzi[11] anticipated that, I had to shift the focus. W. Warren Wagar alarmed me again, but his book[12] turned out to deal with a later phase of Wells. Fortunately for my peace of mind, the Mark Hillegas book, devoted mostly to the influence of Wells' anti-utopian fiction, did not appear until 1967.

Most of this first version was published as a series of five articles in Leland Sapiro's *Riverside Quarterly* (August, 1967 to August, 1969). The manuscript was also offered to a series of university presses. Some of them wrote encouraging reports and held it for periods of a year or longer, but they all finally turned it down.

The reasons given for rejection varied from shortage of funds to an opinion that it should have said more about Wagar—whose fine book deals with another side of Wells altogether. A more substantial reason, I imagine, is the fact that the universities, until recently, have seldom been concerned with science fiction by Wells or anybody else. I like Sir Charles Snow's explanation of their attitude.[13]

His notion of the two cultures is probably another over-simplification, but I think it does point to a very real difference in contemporary views of the world. Wells' shifting allegiance to the culture of science must be left for a later section of this book, but here it seems pertinent to comment that the university is one strong fortress of the traditional literary academic culture, which has always been slow to accept science fiction or Wells himself.

Remarkably, however, in the past few years, science fiction has begun to establish a beachhead in the university.[14] In the preliminary survey already noted, I discovered more than 200 academic courses in science fiction, ranging from the freshman to the graduate levels. Such developments no doubt encouraged my present publisher to accept this book.

I hope that it may be admitted to the still-slender list of useful critical works on science fiction. Perhaps because the *genre* has been identified with the culture of science, most literary critics have either ignored or misunderstood it. Professional scholars have generally dismissed Wells' early work as mere entertainment, cleverly written but intellectually insignificant.

Much of the really informed and relevant criticism of science fiction, in fact, has originally appeared in such fan magazines as *Riverside Quarterly* and *Speculation,* with circulations under a thousand copies, or in the science fiction pulps. Two of the most knowledgeable and penetrating books available, Damon Knight's *In Search of Wonder* (Chicago, 1967), and William Atheling's (James Blish's) *The Issue at Hand* (Chicago, 1964), have been collected from such sources.

A few other books of intelligent criticism have been produced by science fiction writers. Among them are *Modern Science Fiction: Its Meaning and Its Future,* edited by Reginald Bretnor (New York, 1953); *The Science Fiction Novel,* introduced by Basil Davenport (Chicago, 1959); and *Of Worlds Beyond* (edited by Lloyd Arthur Eshbach (Reading, Pa., 1947). Robert Silverberg's *The Mirror of Infinity: A Critic's Anthology of Science Fiction* (New York, 1970) includes useful essays.

J. O. Bailey's *Pilgrims through Space and Time* (New York, 1947) is valuable for summaries and bibliographies of early work. Thomas Clareson's *SF: The Other Side of Realism* (Bowling Green, 1971) reprints recent essays. The series of volumes by Sam Moskowitz[15] contains masses of useful information, especially on more recent science fiction, though the criticism is sometimes naive and the facts are sometimes inaccurate.

A handful of people outside the field, notably Kingsley Amis in *New Maps of Hell* (New York, 1960), Basil Davenport in *Inquiry into Science Fiction* (New York, 1955), and Robert M. Philmus in *Into the Unknown* (Berkeley, 1970), have written about science fiction with sympathy and understanding. Others might be named, and the growing popularity of science fiction as an academic subject will no doubt lead to more academic writing about it—some may be too academic!—but the list of useful works available now is soon exhausted.

Most of these books are devoted to more recent science fiction, especially to that produced since 1926, when the magazines began to define and promote it as a special *genre*. Wells commonly receives a bow of respect but seldom any real examination. His recognition by such scholars as Bergonzi and Hillegas is only a start. As the chief creator of modern science fiction, he is surely due more critical attention than he has yet received.

The spectacular rise and fall of his literary reputation will be outlined in more detail in the following chapter. The science fiction was the first foundation of his vast popularity. Though his later work was once familiar everywhere, most of it is topical journalism, propaganda for the world state, or popular education. The science fiction was done before he gave up his art to champion great causes. It has always been widely read, and I believe it deserves another appreciation, besides those of Bergonzi and Hillegas.

To paraphrase the dissertation abstract, this book is devoted to the premise that Wells' early science fiction presents a searching and significant criticism of the idea of progress. The idea, though formally buried long ago by intellectuals hostile to the culture of science, is still alive in the minds of many men all over the world, in uncriticized forms that seem responsible for many of the tensions that make today's headlines.

Wells' literary reputation has suffered by association with the cult of progress. Identified as the great utopian of his age, he has been stereotyped and unfairly denigrated as the deluded prophet of a crassly materialistic progress. With better justice, the early Wells might have been welcomed among the skeptics of progress in Snow's traditional literary culture. Though obsessed with change, he never expected it to pour out unearned benefits, either material or moral.

His attitudes, true, as we trace them through the fiction, appear to have been complex and shifting. We discover an internal conflict that seems to reflect the clash of modern science against the conservative rural middle-class traditions of his early environment, as well as the more primitive clash of self against society. Since he had found his most vital literary material in this inner struggle, he was crippled as a writer by its partial solution in the early stories. Later, however, with many of his first doubts of progress left behind, he emerged from the conflict to become the great spokesman of his time for the culture of science.

This searching criticism of the idea of progress seems likely to take first place among Wells' considerable intellectual achievements. He had learned from T. H. Huxley to see mankind as a biological species subject to the laws of evolution. Defining progress as successful adaptive change, he used his early stories to dramatize both the external limits set by the nature of the cosmos and the internal limits set by the biological nature of man. He saw that adaptive success is necessarily relative to environment, and that ethical ideals are consequently irrelevant to the evolutionary process—a position that may go far to account for his rejection by members of the traditional literary culture.

Somewhat arbitrarily, I have divided Wells' science fiction novels and stories into three groups. *The Time Machine* (1895) and *The War of the Worlds* (1898) emphasize the external or cosmic limits to human progress. *The Island of Dr. Moreau* (1896) and *The Invisible Man* (1897) stress the internal biological limits, those due to our animal past. *When the Sleeper Wakes* (1899) and *The First Men in the Moon* (1901) document the relativity and the moral ambiguity of such change as does take place.

Beneath all the color and adventure and appealing humanity of Wells' science fiction, we find a pessimistic critique of pure reason and absolute ethics. Composing his stories as dramatic tests of the idea of progress, he finds that our future advancement is limited not only by our own nature and by the conditions of an uncaring cosmos, but also by a self-defeated mechanism inherent in the evolutionary process. He finds that science, uncontrolled by social tradition, is both destructive and self-destructive. The "optimism" of his later years seems to have been no inconsistent shift of attitude, but rather a quietly desperate attempt to alert mankind and lead us safely past the limits he had so vividly foreseen.

My special thanks are due to several of the people who made this book possible. To Adolph L. Soens, a science fiction fan who agreed to sponsor an academic study of Wells. To Lewis Sawin and Leslie L. Lewis, scholars and friends who helped me to complete it. To David Hawkins and Edmond Hamilton, who suggested important materials. To Leland Sapiro, for able editing and first publication. To Jack Chalker, for the rescue of a hope that had begun to seem forlorn. To Blanche, my wife, for aid that passes understanding.

The Liberation of a Mind

1 The Prophet and his Honor

In a curious way, H. G. Wells is immortal. The physical organism, under-sized and squeaky-voiced and generally inadequate, died in 1946. The serious literary artist had perished thirty years before, a martyr to great causes. Yet Wells himself lives on, in a multitude of conflicting images.

Not only the prodigal father of modern science fiction, he is the international statesman who devoted most of his life to the dream of a new world order.[1] He is the little Englishman who earned a welcome in the White House and the Kremlin.[2] He is the long-forgotten prophet of the masses, the universal pundit whose snap judgements once sold for a dollar a word. He is the atheist who hated God,[3] the evangelist of a deified Spirit of Man,[4] the zealot who tried to write a new Bible.[5] He is the cockney Don Juan, the tenderly devoted husband revealed in *The Book of Catherine Wells*,[6] the loving father who wrote "The Magic Shop"[7] to entertain his son. He is the facile popular journalist who learned from a book by J. M. Barrie how to write glittering trivia,[8] the literary artist once admired by Henry James, the dedicated and inspiring teacher whose classroom finally included most of the world.[9] He is the visionary optimist who wrote *A Modern Utopia*,[10] and also the critical pessimist who challenged every

19

theory of progress.

Even other images are current, but the Wells who criticizes progress is the one who demands attention, for strong reasons. An essential part of the whole man, this image has been too commonly overlooked. It points the way to a consistent pattern beneath all the other images. More than any other image of Wells, it is relevant to us. For the idea of progress is immortal, in the same curious way that Wells is. In the mind of the literary intellectual, it withered and died about the end of the nineteenth century, blighted by the *fin de siècle* pessimism of Oscar Wilde and Aubrey Beardsley and Max Nordeau.[11] In other minds all over the world, however, the hope of progress remains alive and vigorous, in shapes as numerous and contradictory as the surviving images of Wells. It survives in the five-year plans of Communism, in the new nationalism of the colonial peoples, in all the aspirations of the West—even in the investment of many billion dollars to realize the old Wellsian dream of a voyage to the moon. Everywhere, it stands in need of the kind of criticism that Wells expresses in his first fiction.

During his own physical life, his reputation blazed and faded like a literary comet. He earned a quick and immense success with the half-dozen scientific romances that began with *The Time Machine* in 1895. Turning gradually from literary art to pamphleteering journalism, he averaged more than two books a year for fifty years. Long before his death, his fame had gone into eclipse, for reasons now clear enough. His cockney pride and his restless impatience with things as they were had annoyed every sort of conservative. As the voiciferous spokesman of his generation for what C. P. Snow calls the culture of science, he had alienated the literary intellectuals.[12] His campaign for a new world order had found no effective support. His great popular textbooks on history and biology and social science were going out of date. Only the early fiction and one or two of his comic novels were still widely read.

Although Wells is too large to be readily shelved for oblivion, the effort has been made. His work has been neatly catalogued in three periods: the scientific romances (1895-1900), the comedies (1900-1910), and the novels of ideas (after 1910), with the comment that "the work of the last phase can be ignored."[13] In the imaginative stories of the early period, he was a new Robert Louis Stevenson or H. Rider Haggard or Jules Verne.[14] In the comedies of the middle period he was another Dickens.[15] In the voluminous journalism of the last period, he was a second Defoe, adept at sugar-coating his facts and sermons with convincing circumstantial detail. A confident prophet of social progress, he persistently under-estimated the irrational elements in man.[16]

Such statements contain some truth, but they can explain neither the place of Wells in his own generation nor his relevance today. The division of his work into three periods is too neat to be accurate. As late as 1937, with *The Croquet Player,* he is still writing Stevensonian allegory; the vein of comedy runs through all his books from the time an angel is brought down with a fowling piece in *The Wonderful Visit* (1895)—even from the time he wrote *The Desert Daisy,* about 1879;[17] all his novels are novels of ideas. A glance into the early fiction is enough to shatter the image of Wells as the foolish optimist who died embittered by the failure of his dream of easy progress. *The Time Machine,* his first novel, places all its gloomy emphasis on the retrograde evolution and final extinction of the human race.

Although this image of "crass Wellsianism"[18] has become a critical stereotype, Wells was once widely understood. Louis Cazamian, for example, has given him an acute evaluation. "Impulsive as it is . . . his thought is none the less one of the most substantial in contemporary Europe. . . . What a Balzac and a Zola had done in France, Wells does again in England . . . with a sociological sense more precise than that of either."[19] In the opinion of Anatole France, *"Il est le plus intelligent des Anglais!"*[20] Leo J. Henkin, in his lucid study of *Darwinism in the English Novel: 1860-1910,*[21] recognizes Wells' unique combination of scientific insight and literary power, and discusses "the idea of degeneration" in Wells' early fiction.[22] He concludes that "though his work is a milestone in the history of evolutionary romance there were few with the grounding in science and the vivid and fluent imagination to follow him into the future."[23] In spite of such perceptions, however, the image of Wells as the critic of progress was almost lost for a whole generation. Only recently has it come back into the focus of attention.

The new appreciation of Wells began with an important article by his son, Anthony West, published in 1957. West names George Orwell and St. John Ervine as examples of "the new obscurantists" who have upheld the false image of Wells as "a mind led away to folly and despair by the nineteenth century progressive fallacy, and by a blind faith in science."[24] Defending his father, West cites Wells' own essay, "The Rediscovery of the Unique,"[25] his first important published work, which shows that even at the beginning of his career he had rejected the idea of unlimited evolutionary progress. West concedes that Wells did have an optimistic phase, beginning about 1900, when success had brought him out of the rural and proletarian worlds in which he had grown up, and into contact with men of wealth and intelligence who were also men of good will. Wells found a temporary prop for this optimism in the Pragmatism of William James, but when that failed his early pessimism returned to overwhelm his progressive idealism. His last despair, West believes, was not due to any disappointment in mankind, but rather to remorse for his own failure as an artist to express the virile stoicism that had made his life happy and creative in spite of his pessimism. "He had known the worst there is for man to know about himself and his fate from the beginning, and he had faltered only in sharing his knowledge." [26]

In the few years since, the old stereotype of Wells as the disappointed prophet of an automatic sort of progress has been hidden in a flurry of new recognition. The University of Illinois has acquired the Wells papers, and the University of Illinois Press is publishing his letters. [27] A beginning has been reported on a full-length biography. An H. G. Wells Society is devoted to the revival of his socialistic and utopian thought. [28] Besides *H. G. Wells and the World State,* W. Warren Wagar's study of Wells as the evangelist and champion of the coming global society, several other important books have appeared.

Writing from a literary point of view, in *The Early H. G. Wells,* Bernard Bergonzi has done a sensitive analysis of the conflicts and ambivalences that Wells reveals in the scientific romances. A student of science fiction, Mark Hillegas has traced the international influence of Wells' early work, in *The Future as Nightmare: H. G. Wells and the Anti-Utopians.* Lovat Dickson has published a new biography, *H. G. Wells: His Turbulent Life and Times,* (New York, 1969) notable chiefly for what it says about the private life of the later Wells—his own *Experiment in Autobiography* is a remarkably candid account of his life from the beginning down through the years when he was writing his great science fiction.

This present book seeks to show the essential unity of Wells' work more fully, and to show more precisely his place in the thought of our time, through a new survey of his treatment of the idea of progress. No idea, of course, is ever quite the same in two different minds, and Wells' notion of progress is by no means the same idea preached by Comte or by Marx or even by Herbert Spencer. In the mind of Wells, the idea was not only defined by his knowledge of biology, but it was additionally controlled by his realistic knowledge of human nature. In his scheme of thought, the progressive idealism of the nineteenth century came into conflict with a classical attitude derived in part from his reading of such writers as Swift and Johnson and Voltaire, and doubtless in greater part from the social environment of his early life.

This conflict within the mind of Wells, especially as it is revealed through the early fiction, will be the focal point of this study. Perhaps every artist is at odds with himself; and indeed, at some stage of his life, so is every human being. In the case of Wells, this internal quarrel is the key to his essential character and to the facts of his life. It gives shape and substance to the early science fiction, which seems to have served as a sort of imaginative laboratory in which Wells was testing discrepant ideas and attitudes. The conflict arises from the facts of change, and the criticism of the idea of progress emerges as a central symbol for deeper and more personal divisions of mind.

2   Theories of Progress

Permanence and change are two poles which exert conflicting forces not only upon Wells but upon each of us. As Whitehead puts it: "There are two principles inherent in the very nature of things, recurring in some particular embodiments whatever field we explore—the spirit of change, and the spirit of conservation."[29] The manifestations of this conflict are too nearly universal to be enumerated, and most of the psychological and anthropological and philosophical implications lie beyond the scope of this study. Yet the basic idea opens useful insights into Wells and his relevance to modern man.

The idea of progress is the symbol of change in the thought of Wells, and his early fiction records a bitterly critical reaction against it. The details of this struggle will appear as the separate works are discussed.

The scope and importance of the idea of progress scarcely needs emphasis. The fact of change is as universal as the human hunger for permanence. The polarity between the two determines character and channels attitudes, all the way from the first clash of the individual infant with its mother as the figure of society, to the last defense of the aging conservative against the resurgent liberalism of a new generation. Change arises largely from the inner nature of the individual; permanence is sought outside the individual, especially in the structure of society.[30]

The progressive idealism that Wells questions so searchingly in the early fiction was an idea of the nineteenth century, supported by an optimistic interpretation of Darwin's biological theory of evolution and by the even more optimistic implications of Herbert Spencer's general evolutionary theory. But optimism and even ideas of evolution are almost as old as the fact of change. Arthur O. Lovejoy and George Boas, in their monumental *Primitivism and Related Ideas in Antiquity*,[31] have collected many anticipatory notions of progress—notions that were always overwhelmed in the ancient world by primitivistic concepts of steady or cyclic degeneration. J. B. Bury, defining progress as the belief that "civilisation has moved, is moving, and will move in a desirable direction,"[32] has traced the evolution of the idea from its first intimations among the Hebrews and the Greeks to its climax at the end of the nineteenth century.

Such ideas cannot flourish except in favorable climates of opinion. Ideas of progress require a climate of civilization. Among primitive men, social change is too slow to be apparent. The revolution of the seasons and the succession of the generations may suggest naive notions of cyclic change, lost childhoods may be reflected in legends of a golden age, and individual aging may give rise to theories of decay, but unlettered men lack any permanent points of reference from which to measure progressive change. The concept of the world as process requires sophistication. The primitive man lacks both Wells' sense of the unity of mankind, and Wells' confidence in the significance of human life on earth. The idea of progress found no favorable climate in classical times, or during the Middle Ages. When a favorable climate was at last established, by the thought of such men as Sir Francis Bacon,[33] Descartes,[34] and Leibnitz,[35] the idea burst promptly into flower.

The French Revolution, as historians from the time of De Tocqueville have perceived, was a sort of holy war, its banner the idea of progress. Its militant faith overflowed frontiers, sustained by its own dogmas and rituals and saints, "by a mystical faith in humanity, in the ultimate regeneration of the human race."[36] This new religion had already crossed the Channel, a good century before the birth of Wells, though its effects were less explosive in England than in France. Adam Smith in his *Wealth of Nations* (1776) assumes a gradual economic progress resulting from the economic unity of the human race. Priestley wrote that, "whatever was the beginning of this world, the end will be glorious and paradisiacal beyond what our imaginations can now conceive."[37] William Godwin's *Political Justice* (1793), for all its attacks upon political authority and social institutions, proclaimed the perfectibility of mankind.

At this point, the doctrine of unlimited progress was challenged by Malthus, whose *Essay on the Principle of Population* (1798) started a conflicting train of thought which ran on through the minds of Darwin and Wallace, where it led to the theory of natural selection,[38] and down through the lectures and essays of T. H. Huxley, and finally to the sardonic rejection of evolution as an instrument of any ideal kind of progress in Wells' *The Island of Dr. Moreau.*[39]

From the beginning of the nineteenth century, the evolving concepts of progress took two directions.[40] In one branch of development, Comte and Owen and Marx each worked out a blueprint for a particular society designed to perfect human nature. When this millenial state had been achieved, all change was to stop—except perhaps for some inconsequential additions to art or to knowledge. Actually, such ideas return to the pagan tradition of the slow degeneration of an ideal state founded by a wise legislator. Once such a state is established, as it has been in Soviet Russia, it tends to become in most respects intensely conservative. Change is admitted only within the very narrow limits allowed by the founders of the state.

Theories in the other line of development place no limit upon progressive change. The state remains the servant of the people, not the master. The consequent political philosophy is a broad liberalism. Individual liberty is both the goal and the instrument of social advances, which may continue indefinitely. The theories of Godwin, John Stuart Mill, and Herbert Spencer belong here. So do the ideas of the mature H. G. Wells, when he had passed the critical period of the early fiction.

In the decade after 1848, the theory of progress entered what Bury calls the third stage of its history.[41] In the first stage, before the French Revolution, there had been only casual anticipations of the notion of progress. In the second stage, such thinkers as Comte had searched for a law of progress. In the third stage, the theory of evolution provided not only a plausible explanation but also an apparent proof of progress. Bury dates this stage from 1859, when Darwin's *Origin of Species* appeared; just as accurately he might have dated it from Spencer's essay, "Progress: Its Law and Cause," first published in *Westminster Review* in April, 1857.[42]

All the accumulating evidences of evolution were also

evidences of past progress. Although T. H. Huxley made no claim that social evolution must increase individual happiness, Darwin saw fit to conclude his *Origin of Species* on an optimistic note:

> As all the living forms of life are the lineal descendants of those which lived long before the Cambrian epoch, we may feel certain that the ordinary succession by generation has never once been broken, and that no cataclysm has desolated the whole world. Hence we may look with some confidence to a secure future of some length. And as natural selection works solely by and for the good of each being, all corporal and mental endowments will tend to progress toward perfection.[43]

It is this view of progress that Wells questions in *The Time Machine* and *The Island of Dr. Moreau*.

Spencer's theory of evolution is broader than Darwin's, and even more optimistic. The evolution of life is only a special case of the general process he describes in *First Principles*:

> Evolution is the integration of matter and the concomitant dissipation of motion; during which the matter passes from an indefinite, incoherent homogeneity to a definite, coherent heterogeneity; and during which the retained motion undergoes a parallel transformation.[44]

Like Comte, Spencer tries to build a complete system of thought upon the scientific method. His purpose is ambitious; the smooth order of his imagined world-machine is still impressive. Yet his influence upon Wells would be hard to trace. Their ideas of progress were sharply different, and Wells' own comments on Spencer are often critical. Certainly the influence of Darwin and Huxley was more direct, but Spencer's optimistic philosophy was part of the intellectual climate into which the maturing mind of Wells emerged.

Wells neither borrowed nor invented any vast system of thought. He criticized the universal schemes of Comte and Marx even more severely than he did Spencer's. The idea of progress that he carried out of the critical period was his own, planted by other minds but shaped by the harsh facts of his own life. He has acknowledged the influence of Huxley, "the acutest observer, the ablest generalizer, . . . the most lucid and valiant of controversialists."[45] He writes that the day when he walked across Kensington Gardens to begin his studies at the Normal School of Science was one of the great days of his life. The study of zoology under Huxley "was a grammar of form and a criticism of fact. That year I spent in Huxley's class, was beyond all question, the most educational year of my life."[46]

But Wells was eighteen by then. He had already glimpsed the possibility of social progress, in Plato's *Republic* and Henry George's *Progress and Poverty*.[47] Even earlier, his brain had been sensitized by the spark of nonconformity in his cricketeering father, by the severe but genteel poverty of his home behind the failing shop at Atlas House, by his close acquaintance with the anachronistic eighteenth-century squirearchy at Up Park, by his sufferings as an unwilling draper's apprentice.

Progress, for Wells, was never the universal law of Comte's Positivism, nor the historic logic of Marx's dialectical materialism, nor even the benign force of Spencer's evolution. His most splendid dreams of better possible worlds were always curbed by the stubborn respect for fact that he had learned from Huxley, and by the realistic awareness of human imperfections that he had gained from his own unsheltered life. In his later optimistic period, he believed that he had found "the pattern of the key to master our world and release its imprisoned promise."[48] But even then Wells was never the "cosmic optimist" as Perry Miller uses that phrase to describe the Puritan who held that "if the creation is ruled by God's will, and His will is itself the norm of justice and equity, the universe must be essentially good,"[49] nor even as Conner uses it to mean "the interpretation of evolution as a progress that is inevitable because in some sense it is divinely motivated."[50]

Even the later Wells was always more the cosmic pessimist than the cosmic optimist. As he confesses in the autobiography, his attempt to deify the spirit of man in *Mr. Britling Sees it Through* (1916) and the following novels was never much more than a stirring metaphor.[51] He warns that progress will require "incessant toil . . . sacrifice . . . and much fearless conflict."[52] He sees advancement never as the unfolding of a divine plan or as the operation of some obscurely benevolent metaphysical process, but simply as the possible but uncertain result of ordinary biological processes brought under intelligent human control. All his life he refused to believe "that the order of nature has any bias in favor of man than it had in favor of the ichyosaur or the pterodactyl."[53] However inspiring, his visions of progress are always glimpses of a possible reward to be earned by reason and courage and effort; they are never promises of an unearned bounty to come from some friendly law of nature.

His idea of progress can be defined more clearly by comparison with the rival ideas of Comte and Marx and Spencer. He writes in the autobiography:

> Probably I am unjust to Comte and grudge to acknowledge a sort
> of priority he had in sketching the modern outlook. But for him,
> as for Marx, I have a real personal dislike, a genuine reluctance
> to concede him any sort of leadership. It is I think part of an
> inherited dislike of leadership and a still profounder objection to
> the subsequent deification of leaders.[54]

In a "discourse delivered to the Royal Institution on January 24,
1902," printed as *The Discovery of the Future*, he repudiates
the Positivist doctrine with a characteristic vigor, emphasizing
Comte's ignorance of the prehistoric past and the "peculiar limitations of the Positivist conception of the future."[55] Since
Darwin has trained our imaginations upon a longer view of the
past than Comte saw, we now see that modern man

> is no more than the present phase of a development so great and
> splendid that, beside this vision, epics jingle like nursery rhymes,
> and all the exploits of Humanity shrivel to the proportions of
> castles in the sand.[56]

Wells rejected the ideas of Marx just as explicitly. His own
socialism, he says, was pre-Marxist. He had "scarcely heard the
name of Karl Marx" before he came to London, where his biological training soon equipped him to find the flaws in Marx's
"plausible, mystical and dangerous idea of reconstituting the
world on a basis of mere resentment and destruction."[57] There
might have been "creative revolution of a far finer type if Karl
Marx had never lived." This vigorous opposition to Marxism must
have come partly from Wells' keen awareness that he belonged to
a middle class. His parents had been servants, but upper servants, not proletarians. He was grateful for the class feeling he
was taught at Mr. Thomas Morley's Academy, which was a middle-
class school "saturated with the spirit of individual self-reliance
and individual dignity.[58]

The Marxists, on their side, knew him for a stranger. After
his interview with Lenin in 1920, according to Trotsky, Lenin
said vehemently: "What a bourgeois he is! He is a philistine! Ah,
what a philistine!"[59] Marxist critics have commented upon his
lack of sympathy with the proletariat: the proletarian Morlocks
are evil monsters in *The Time Machine,* and even in "A Story of
the Days to Come" and *When the Sleeper Wakes* he rejects the
idea that the exploited workers can help themselves.[60] Wells'
pride of class helped to protect him from the Marxist dogma of
limited progress toward a limited and arbitrary goal, and supported the sturdy independence which inclined him toward at
least a hope for perpetual human progress.

With Herbert Spencer, Wells had more in common. Both men shared the same liberal belief in the possibility of indefinite evolution toward an always happier human race living free in an ever more perfect society. Both were scientists, rather than utopians; both were aware that evolution is controlled by natural forces acting in a cosmos neither created nor operated for the benefit of man. Both saw progress as a possible but uncertain reward for human effort, and both promoted education as the way to advancement. The essays collected in Spencer's *Education*[61] may be read as a kind of prospectus for the later work of Wells, especially for his great trilogy, *The Outline of History* (1920), *The Science of Life* (1931), and *The Work, Wealth, and Happiness of Mankind* (1932), with which he was trying to train good citizens for the coming world state.

To summarize, Wells is more nearly a follower of Spencer than of Marx or Comte. Both Wells and Spencer accept progress as an evolutionary process, which cannot continue without the aid of human intelligence, and which must at last be ended by cosmic forces beyond any possible human control. But Wells, even in his most buoyant years, is less optimistic than Spencer, and the Wells of the early fiction is sharply critical of Spencerian optimism. The influence of T. H. Huxley was always greater than Spencer's.

As a student under Huxley, Wells had learned to see progress as successful adaptation to environment, through variation and survival of the fittest. But Wells rejected the ethical system that Huxley was attempting to erect upon the facts of biology in such essays as "Evolution and Ethics."[62] Instead, in what Anthony West calls "a kind of treason"[63] to Huxley, Wells shows in *The Time Machine* and other stories that values and standards based upon biological fact are pragmatic, relativistic, and entirely irrelevant to the happiness and freedom and fulfillment of the individual.

In the sanguine period that began in the first decade of this century, Wells did not renounce Darwinism; he turned instead from the stoic pessimism of Huxley's interpretation[64] to the more optimistic reading suggested by Darwin himself.[65] Even his later views are sharply distinct from the creative evolution of Samuel Butler and Bergson.[66] Butler satirizes Darwinism in *Erewhon*,[67] and in his four books on evolution,[68] he reverts to a mystical neo-Lamarckism, attempting to substitute inherited memory and creative will for the role of chance in natural selection.[69]

A steadfast Darwinian, Wells stresses the factor of chance.[70] Except in his metaphorical deification of the human spirit, he avoids mysticism. He simply sees the expanding human intelligence as a new element in the evolutionary process. Understanding the mechanism of evolutionary progress, the human mind can hope to control it. Reason can depose blind chance, in a simpler and more obvious way than Butler suggests, and human purpose can now reach for control of the universe. It is this biological, rather than mystical, view of progress which informs all the later efforts of Wells to educate and organize the citizens of the new world republic. He writes optimistically in *The Science of Life*:

> It is clear that what man can do with wheat and maize may be done with every living species in the world—including his own. . . . Once the eugenic phase is reached, humanity may increase very rapidly in skill, mental power, and general vigor.[71]

Theories of change have continued to evolve since the time of T. H. Huxley and the early Wells. Mendel's rediscovered work has revealed part of the mechanism of biological change. Freud has illuminated the dynamics of change in the individual. Current anthropology is offering more precise descriptions of change.[72] In general, scientific progress continues at an exponential rate, while social progress totters along the brink of catastrophe.

3   Patterns of Rebellion

Wells understood man's war with himself. In the preface to the second volume of the Atlantic Edition, he says that *The Island of Dr. Moreau*[73] was a response to the reminder in a scandalous trial of the time [that of Oscar Wilde][74] "that humanity is but animal rough-hewn to a reasonable shape and in perpetual internal conflict between instinct and injunction."[75] Nor was Wells himself exempt. As we speculated in the opening chapter, the criticism of progress in Wells' science fiction is probably symbolic of an inner conflict too deep and too complex to be briefly analyzed. In the beginning it must have been the self against society. *The Invisible Man*[76] presents the case for society: Griffin's story is a parable of the selfish individualist hunted down and destroyed because he will not conform to the terms of society. "The Country of the Blind"[77] presents the opposing case for the individual: Nuñez finds death upon the mountain snows preferable to the sacrifices required by social conformity.

The conflict is also the past against the future. In a whole group of short stories, such as "Aepyornis Island"[78] and "The Land Ironclads,"[79] the modern world is in conflict with the primitive past. In *The War of the Worlds,*[80] a symbolic future lays waste to the present with military armor, poison gas, and weapons that are clearly thermonuclear. Wells begins *The Discovery of the Future* by describing two divergent and conflicting types of mind, the retrospective or submissive, which seeks only "to reap the consequences of the past,"[81] and the constructive or creative, "which is perpetually attacking and altering the established order of things, perpetually falling away from what the past has given us."[82] As he wrote the early science fiction, his own mind was shifting toward the second type.

His inner conflict, in another sense, is classicism against romanticism. In a preface to a collection of the early romances, he stresses his "early, profound, and lifelong admiration for Swift,"[83] but in a discussion of his attitudes toward sex and marriage he acknowledges the influence of Shelley.[84] Though the plot materials of the scientific fantasies may appear wildly romantic, the critical attitudes toward progress are sternly classic. In Wells' impatience with traditional literary forms, shown in his abandonment of the short story about the date of "The Country of the Blind" (1903), in his efforts to invent a new and more elastic form for the novel,[85] and in his literary debate with Henry James,[86] there is evidence of a gradual victory of romantic individualism over classic restraint.

His conflict is the country against the city: Up Park against London. It is the upper classes against the proletariat: the Eloi against the Morlocks in *The Time Machine,*[87] Ostrog against the wearers of the blue in *When the Sleeper Wakes.*[88] Wells mistrusts the masses, and he anticipates the rise of a new aristocracy (modeled upon the guardians of Plato's Republic) in his vision of the Samurai in *A Modern Utopia* (1905). He writes in the autobiography:

> A Samurai Order educated in such an ideology as I have since tried to shape out, is inevitable if the modern world-state is ever to be fully realized.[89]

Though he has no use for the class of social parasites, a stubborn contempt for democracy runs through his work.

Wells' conflict is religion against atheism. In the autobiography he has vividly recorded his struggles to escape the vengeful primitive God of his childhood,[90] but he never fully outgrew the emotions and attitudes of religion, which appear in his efforts to deify the mind of the race, and again in his years of religious devotion to the cause of a new world order. His most scathing satire against conventional religion is in *The Island of Dr. Moreau*.[91]

His conflict in yet another sense is conservatism against liberalism: his home and his first schools against the scientific method and the ideas of socialism. It is permanence against progress: the comfortable security of things as they are against the exciting promise of things that would be better. Plato's *Republic,* "a very releasing book" which he read at Up Park before he went to London, had filled his mind with ideas of change.

> Here was the amazing and heartening suggestion that the whole fabric of law, custom and worship, which seemed so invincibly established, might be cast into the melting pot and made anew.[92]

His revolutionary ideas of economics and government, of sex and religion, came from Plato rather than from Marx.

The most striking thread of his inner conflict, a common theme in most of the early science fiction, is intellect against emotion. The Invisible Man is selfish intellect. The Martians in *The War of the Worlds* are exaggerated intellect, almost disembodied. Dr. Moreau is emotionless intelligence. The Grand Lunar, in *The First Men in the Moon*,[93] is a brain evolved to the ultimate. Ostrog, in *When the Sleeper Wakes,* is political cunning unrestrained by moral feelings. Even the Morlocks possess a kind of intelligence. In none of these stories does pure reason lead toward individual happiness or toward any ideal social goal. Instead, it forces the individual toward suffering, deprivation, and death.[94] Man's reason, as Wells wrote in 1891, is "about as much a truth-seeking tool as the snout of a pig."[95]

This sustained criticism of man's intellect is the most damaging attack upon the idea of progress in the early fiction. It is fundamental. The whole theory of creative evolution, as Wells later accepted it, is that the emerging human mind will replace blind and random cosmic forces in control of the evolutionary process. Human reason is to assume the creative role ascribed once to God, and later to natural selection. But Wells shows emphatically in the early fiction that the mind of man is utterly unfit to guide progress in any ideal direction, because it is inevitably only one cog in a cosmic machine that is entirely indifferent to ethical values.

A more timely aspect of Wells' internal struggle is the clash between science and humanism, now familiar in the phrase of C. P. Snow as "the conflict of the two cultures."[96] Though

Snow's feud with his humanistic critics is recent, the quarrel itself is old. Plato may even have given Wells his first intimations of the issue, with the animadversions against the poet in his *Republic* (II, X). Thomas Henry Huxley[97] and Matthew Arnold[98] were debating the question in the 1880's, and Wells himself discussed it with George Gissing during the years when he was writing the early fiction.[99] This side of Wells' struggle with himself will be discussed more fully in the last chapter of this book.

In simpler terms, Wells' conflict is pessimism against optimism. It is even a matter of youth against age, hope against illness, and success against failure. His desperate struggle for sheer survival is enough to explain a good part of his early pessimism; his brilliant success with the early fiction brought health and fame and his brightest optimism; the slow ebbing away of time and creative vigor brought a returning pessimism that increased until he died. Partly it is no more than something that was floating in the air: the intellectual skepticism and the fatalistic gloom of what Bergonzi calls the *fin du globe* myth,[100] against a cheerful vitality that supported an unquenchable hope for better things.

However this conflict is described, it must have originated partly in the contrasts and tensions between Wells' own parents. In the autobiography, his mother dominates the early years. She had been a ladies' maid before her marriage; she drudged for twenty-four years in the "dismal unsanitary hole" of the cramped home behind the unsuccessful crockery shop called Atlas House; she later returned to Up Park as housekeeper. Devoutly religious, she never escaped or wanted to escape the ideas of her time and class. The "vast unexpected forces" of progress presented themselves to her "as a series of perplexing frustrations and undeserved misfortunes, for which nothing or nobody was clearly to blame—unless it was my father."[101] She toiled and prayed for her sons, and strove to make them conform. With no grasp of the unfolding aspirations of Wells, she was bent on making him a draper. Loving him, she was yet the stupid, stubborn antagonist of his emerging ideas of progress.

Wells presents his father, son of the head gardener to Lord de Lisle at Penhurst Place in Kent, as a genial but futile individualist. He had lost a series of situations as gardener or undergardener, perhaps because "he did not like to be told things and made to do things."[102] He had talked of migrating to Australia or America. An active athletic man, he spent more time at professional

bowling and cricket than in the shop. He "read diversely" and
encouraged his son to read.

> His was a mind of inappeasable freshness, in the strangest con-
> trast to my mother's. I do not think my mother ever had a new
> idea after she left Miss Riley's school; her ideas faded out, that
> was all. But my father kept going to the last.[103]

Oddly, in the biography by Geoffrey West (which Wells calls
"exact and careful")[104] the images of the parents are almost
reversed. The mother shrinks and the father expands.

> For thirty years Joe Wells was a ubiquitous and popular figure in
> Bromley, with his ruddy sun-burnt complexion, short crisp beard,
> curling grey hair, and jovial bearing. He lingers in peoples' mem-
> ories as dictatorial, having decided opinions and acting upon
> them, and altogether overshadowing his small and much more
> "genteel" wife.[105]

West remarks that Wells has never presented faithful portraits of
his parents, but agrees that Joseph Wells was an intelligent and
stimulating nonconformist, and that Sarah's "respectful acceptance of the established order" was the first great obstacle to the
progress of her son.[106]

That conflict between his parents molded the maturing mind
of Wells into a pattern of rebellion. A brilliant boy, brought up in
an atmosphere of ignorance and inequity and want which his
mother dutifully approved, infected with his father's not unreason-
able discontent, he had no need to wait for Comte or Marx or
Spencer or even for Plato to impart a hope of better things. In
the words of Wells himself, "It was a process of severance and
estrangement, for I was my father's as well as my mother's son."[107]

The pattern of revolt against his mother's illiberalism repeats
itself in every aspect of his life and thought. He revolted against
class inferiority. His mother was a contented servant; sharing his
father's independence, Wells himself became "a typical Cockney
without either reverence or a sincere conviction of inferiority for
any fellow creature."[108] He revolted against his mother's ideas
of God.

> I was indeed a prodigy of Early Impiety. I was scared by Hell, I
> did not at first question at first the existence of Our Father, but
> no fear or terror could prevent my feeling that his All Seeing Eye
> was that of an Old Sneak.[109]

He revolted against his mother's Victorian prudery. She was able
to nip his budding affair with an Up Park kitchen maid named
Mary,[110] but she could not rule his dreams of splendid women or

his ideas of sex freedom. The pattern of sex rebellion appears in his elopement with the student who became his second wife, in his later affairs, in such novels as *Ann Veronica* (1909), in all his speculations about sex and marriage in the new world order. He revolted, too, against economic injustice, and refused to remain a draper's apprentice.

This same pattern of revolt helped to shape Wells' ideas of literary form. He writes that he was caught, early in his career, in a conflict between "the civil service conception of a life framed in devotion to constructive public ends" and the "artistic attitude."[111] In their discussions of the novel, Henry James urged the conventions of literary art, playing somewhat the role of Wells' mother as the champion of tradition. But Wells, as he left the period of the early fiction, was "disposed to regard the novel as about as much an art form as a market place or a boulevard. . . . You went by it on your various occasions."[112] Though his famous clash with James[113] shows nothing of Wells as the critic of progress, it does reveal the later Wells, the spokesman for the culture of science, in a typical misunderstanding with the culture of the literary intellectual.

The men were old friends. James had always admired Wells enough to be distressed by his want of artistic concern. In *Notes on Novelists* (1914) he suggested that

such things as *The New Machiavelli, Marriage, The Passionate Friends*, are . . . very much more attestations of the presence of material than attestations of an interest in the use of it.[114]

Wells retorted to such comments with a caricature and burlesque of James in *Boon,*[115] which is a jumble of bits of satire and serious comment, unorganized and uninhibited, held together only by the transparent pretense that the parts of it are fragments of unfinished work from the pen of George Boon, now dead, who was before the war a popular writer. James, as Geoffrey West puts it,

was naturally distressed to find that art to which he had given his life pilloried and mocked by the one man whom for nearly twenty years he had admired above all others.[116]

Most accounts of the affair have been written by members of the literary culture, who tend to award the victory to James.[117]

But Wells, at least, did not know that he was beaten. The disputing parties, belonging to different cultures, simply did not understand each other. In the correspondence that followed, Wells was forced at one point to admit "that he really didn't know what James was talking about."[118] The basic difference was that

James, as an artist, wanted to render life objectively, as he saw and felt it, without conscious manipulation. The later Wells didn't even care about rendering life; he wanted to change it. Geoffrey West quotes from an introduction he wrote in 1917 to Frank Swinnerton's *Nocturne*: "Personally I have no use at all for life as it is, except as raw material. . . . I have never once 'presented' life. My apparently most objective books are criticisms and incitements to change."[119] Between such fundamental differences, no real contact is possible. Nothing illuminates the nature of the controversy quite so tellingly as Wells' image of what he calls "the elaborate and copious emptiness of the whole Henry James exploit."

> The thing his novel is *about* is always there. It is like a church lit but without a congregation to distract you, with every light and line focused in the high altar. And on the altar, very reverently placed, intensely there, is a dead kitten, an eggshell, a bit of string.[120]

The stress that Wells placed on the role of blind chance in his life is yet another evidence of his Darwinian revolt against the rational world of order and tradition. A childhood accident that broke his leg, he writes in the autobiography, probably saved him from being "a worn-out, dismissed and already dead shop assistant."[121] From the books his father brought him while he was recovering, he got the reading habit. A second broken leg, this time his father's, broke up the precarious household behind the crockery shop, leaving him free to escape another disastrous apprenticeship and to continue his irregular education. He gives credit to the peculiar humor of his Guardian Angel for a ruptured kidney that saved him, in 1887, from becoming "a second rate secondary teacher."[122] Later, his "last cardinal turning point on the road to fortune" was marked by a mouthful of blood.[123] For all the indomitable good humor that Wells displays in this account, such repeated demonstrations of the power of chance can scarcely have supported a faith in the supremacy of human reason or the working of any benevolent law of progress.

4 The Discovery of the Future

This conflict in the mind of Wells had no sudden culmination. His idea of progress must have grown from attitudes as old as his first resentment of his mother as the social instrument restraining his infant egoism. It was always in competition with clashing attitudes, and its predominance in the later work seems to have come from a long process of mental selection and survival of the fittest. Its evolution can be traced through the early work, from the skeptical pessimism that almost overshadows any idea of progress in "The Rediscovery of the Unique" in 1891, to the unfolding optimism of his first parables of unquestioned progress, *The Food of the Gods* (1904) and *In the Days of the Comet* (1906).

Already a highly original thinker in 1891, Wells develops some of the semantic and philosophic and scientific implications of the thesis that "all being is unique." At first, he says, his title was to have been "The Fallacy of the Common Noun"—for the idea of the common noun implies a pattern of identity that does not exist in nature. Anticipating general semantics, he remarks that words are not things, and that no two things are the same. If each event is unique, then change is a constant element in the universe. At the same time, however, that Wells is developing this premise for a theory of progress, he is also foreshadowing the critical attitudes that dominate his early fiction. Progress is possible:

> We are on the eve of man's final emancipation from rigid reasonableness, from the last trace of the trim clockwork thought of the seventeenth and eighteenth centuries.[124]

Human intelligence, unfortunately, is no dependable guide to the future, and science, "a match that man has just got alight," has revealed only a greater darkness.

Anticipations, begun early in 1900 in his new home at Sandgate and first published as a series of magazine articles, reveals his attitudes toward progress in transition from the haunting pessimism of the scientific romances to the expansive optimism of his next phase. The moment seems significant. He is arousing himself from a mood of gloomy intellectual criticism, and methodically forecasting the future history of mankind. His ideas take form as he writes, and here he outlines or suggests most of the themes that are to dominate his future work.

He considers the ways in which human life is controlled by technology, and proceeds to calculate the social results of probable technological advances. When travel is pedestrian, for example, a city has a maximum radius of about four miles; the use of horses increases this to about eight miles; mechanized transportation in the future can increase it indefinitely. Even now, seventy years after its first publication, the book is still exhilarating. Although progress in many fields has outrun Wells' predictions, his vision of the potential greatness of mankind is still inspiring.

Wells himself was excited by the book. He wrote Elizabeth Healey (a bright school companion who remained an affectionate friend):

> *Anticipations* is designed to undermine and destroy the monarch monogamy and respectability—and the British Empire, all under the guise of a speculation about motor cars and electric heating. One has to go quietly in the earlier papers, but the last will be a buster.[125]

Setting out simply to discuss what might happen in the new century, he soon found that he had "a new thing in general thought."[126] More systematically than in the fiction, he was trying "to state and weigh and work out a general resultant of the chief forces of social change in the world."

The book is not fiction. Commonly in fiction, he says, "the provocation of the satirical opportunity has been too much for the writer. The narrative form becomes more and more of a nuisance as the speculative inductions become sincerer."[127] Modern prophecy, he feels, should be "a branch of speculation, and should follow all the decorum of the scientific method."[128] This is the surrender of the literary artist to the more urgent claims of the culture of science.

The future progress that Wells finds revealed by his new method is merely potential, never inevitable. Always aware of the limiting factors in external nature that are beyond human knowledge or control, and also of the more immediately dangerous limiting factors within human nature itself, he sees the future in terms of an evolutionary struggle for existence. The survival of the human race is never certain; he simply feels that it is worth a fight. With this book Wells is beginning the great campaign that lasts through his later life; to warn and educate and unite the race for this struggle to survive.

The essential change that he sees in the future is the collapse of the old class structure and the rise of a new scientific class of technicians and engineers. He places his best hope for progress upon this new culture: the Samurai of *A Modern Utopia* and the members of his later "open conspiracy."[129] Keenly aware of the opposition to be expected from the nonproductive classes, Wells is yet confident that this new culture of "the really functional people" will become the active instrument of progress. Unless civilization is broken down by catastrophe,

> these great kindred groups of capable men and educated, adequate women must be, under the operation of forces we have considered,

the element finally emergent amid the vast confusions of the coming time.[130]

Wells becomes almost mystical about the foreseen triumph of this new class; here is an early hint of his later attempt to deify the human spirit. The construction of the new world order "has an air of being a process independent of any collective or conscious will in man, as being the expression of a greater will."[131] Discussing the education of this new culture, he reveals the seed of purpose that later grew into *The Outline of History* and his other ambitious textbooks for the new world. Since the new class will include emancipated women as well as men, he suggests the revolutionary ideas about sex and marriage that led to such later novels as *Ann Veronica*. Democracy, he feels, is even more likely than marriage to be swept away by the wave of time. It must be eliminated in the course of the evolutionary struggle because of a fatal flaw: democracy leads automatically to war. The new world order will be set up by a "sort of outspoken secret society" of superior men and women.[132]

In *The Discovery of the Future*, Wells returns to this new science of prophecy. He argues that we know the past largely by induction and not by personal observation, and that we should be able to discern the future in the same way. He believes that "we are inclined to underrate our chance of certainties in the future just as . . . we are inclined to be too credulous about the historic past."[133] His old pessimistic bias is reflected in a list of disasters which might logically end the human race, but he rules them out with an admitted act of faith. The book ends upon a note of eloquent optimism that contrasts sharply with the dark mood of the early fiction. "Worlds may freeze and suns may perish, but I believe that there stirs something within us now that can never die again."[134] Even at such moments of exaltation, however, Wells keeps within the limits he has drawn for progress. If we allow for the normal dependence of his moods upon the state of his health and his success in the world, Wells is remarkably consistent in his recognition of these limits. In his optimistic periods he hopes to evade them, but he seldom forgets that they exist. His realistic awareness of the uncertainty of man's fate appears in his first essay, and it still appears in his last almost hopeless book, *The Mind at the End of Its Tether* (1945).

Wells completes this evolution of his thought, from the critic of progress to the evangelist of the new world order, in two of the later romances, *The Food of the Gods*[135] and *In the Days of the Comet*.[136] The first is a parable of progress. As Wells admits, he is transmuting *Anticipations* into fiction, trying to press home the theme that human beings are now faced with changes that require vast readjustments in the scale of their ideas.[137] Though he is still aware of all the difficulties in the way of progress that he had earlier explored, he is saying now that they can be, they must be, overcome—not because the victory will be easy, but because defeat would mean elimination from the struggle to survive. The idea of "big and little men" obviously comes from Swift. The food is an alkaloid that increases the scale of bodily growth six or seven times. The babies who have eaten it grow into forty-foot symbols of the potential greatness that all men might achieve through progress. Their enemies are the little people—physically and intellectually and morally little—who represent various sorts of opposition to progress.

Brilliant in spots, the book should be better than it is. The comic types, the deft satire, and the sharp realism all show Wells' growing novelistic skill. The fantastic symbolism reflects an unfailing power of invention. The narrative is often absorbing, and the poetic visions of man's possible future are inspiring. Yet many readers have found the book disappointing.[138] Perhaps the reason is that Wells had come too near a solution of his own inner conflicts, allowing his attention to shift from the individual to society. Even in *The Desert Daisy* he had been inclined to see people as social types, but the main characters in most of the early fiction are individualized by the projection of his own conflicts. *The Food of the Gods* has no individual hero. The collective hero is the whole new race of giants, standing as a symbol for the idea of progress, and their story sprawls over twenty years, from the invention of the food to their maturity. Though the narrative is vivid and absorbing, the book lacks the dramatic unity and intensity of the earlier romances.

The characters are types. Redwood and Bensington, the inventors of the food, are comic scientists, drawn deliberately small for the sake of contrast with their immense achievement. They exist to make the point that progress is something greater even than the individual men who bring it about. Cossar, "the well-known civil engineer" who leads an expedition against the enormous rats and wasps that have grown from the spilled food, is a typical pioneer of progress, a leader of the culture of science. Possessing energy, courage, and common sense, he uses scientific knowledge to solve problems. He smokes out the giant wasps with sulphur and saltpeter, and ventures bravely down into the holes of the big rats. Yet even he is dwarfed by the children of the food, who are progress itself.

Even before they grow up, the young giants are full of large plans for the future. The three sons of Cossar have a yard where they build huge and powerful new machines. When they leave the yard, however, to build a road for the machines, they are defeated by the property rights of the little men. When they try to set up a great building for the little people, they are frustrated again by "rights and laws and regulations and rascalities" (Bk. III, Ch. I, Sec. 3). Yet, in spite of their defeats, the whole tone of the book is optimistic. Progress is kindled by an increase of human knowledge; it is fed by human intelligence and effort, especially by rational education; but it is a process greater than any human being. The march of greatness must go on, even though individuals drop out.

> In spite of prejudice, in spite of law and regulation, in spite of all the obstinate conservatism that lies at the base of the formal order of mankind, the Food of the Gods, once it had been set going, pursued its subtle and invincible progress (Bk. II, Ch. I, Sec. 1).

The critic of progress has abdicated to the prophet.

The forces opposing progress are illuminated in a series of caricatures, variously comic and sardonic. The first is Bensington's Cousin Jane, a figure of featureless custom and propriety, who refuses to allow him to bring any sort of smelly or wriggly creatures into their flat for scientific purposes, so that he must set up an experimental farm to test the food. The Skinners, the elderly couple employed at the farm, are the comic epitome of all human backwardness, drawn with a Dickensian relish and vigor. Mr. Skinner lisps and has trouble with his buttons and carelessly scatters the food among weeds, insects, and rats. With a kind of animal cunning, Mrs. Skinner steals two tins of the food for her infant grandson.

Anthony West, in fact, suggests that Wells, in his success with the Skinners, has denied his whole progressive theme. The best part of the book is the story of what goes wrong when the food is spilled and scattered, and the Skinners, "monstrous parodies of the average man in their blind sloppiness," are far more believable than the gigantic symbols of progress. Actually, West says,

> the truth is with the Skinners, and what the book convincingly describes is the frustration and the destruction of the progressive grand design by the fallibility of the human material which is necessarily its medium.[139]

Even the giant rats are not only a source of melodramatic action, but also a significant part of the fable. Wells has written elsewhere about the human rodents that

> get the better of us in all sorts of ways and gnaw and scuttle and scamper. They will muck about with our money, misrepresent our purpose and disposition, falsify ownership and waste and frustrate millions of genial lives.[140]

The rats are symbols of the untamed individualist. Like the enormous wasps, they are also reminders that evolution is a race in which every other species is competing, and that the perfection of mankind is not the final purpose of the universe.

As the giant children grow, reaction rises. There is "talk of the bankruptcy of science, of the dying of Progress, of the advent of the Mandarins" (Bk. II, Ch. I, Sec. 1). New opponents of progress appear, among them Lady Wondershoot, who finds the feeding and clothing of the Skinners' gigantic grandson an intolerable burden upon her aristocratic bounty, and sets him to slave for his living in the chalk pit on her estate. In a tragic interlude, the giant rebels against her, smashes the machinery in the pit, and wanders to London, asking questions.

> "What are ye for, ye swarming little people? What are ye all doing—what are ye all for?
>
> "What are ye doing up here, ye swarming little people, while I'm a-cutting chalk for ye, down in the chalk pits there?" (Bk. III, Ch. III, Sec. 2.)

He robs a bread cart, ignores demands that he return to the chalk pit, and is killed at last by the police. But change continues to play with the world; greatness keeps creeping in upon the frightened little men, until the forces of reaction find their leader in a demogogue named Caterham, who leads a movement to stamp out the food and destroy the young giants. The giants resist. At the end one of them stands in their fortress, speaking to his brothers.

> This earth is no resting place, this earth is no resting place, else indeed we might have put our throat to the little people's knife, having no greater right to live than they. And they in turn might yield to the ants and vermin. We fight not for ourselves but for growth, growth that goes on forever. Tomorrow, whether we live or die, growth will conquer through us. That is the law of the spirit forever more. To grow according to the will of God! . . . Till the earth is no more than a footstool (Bk. III, Ch. V, Sec. 3).

The psychological conflict symbolized in Wells' criticism of the idea of progress is essentially the universal clash between ego and environment. This conflict gives the tone and tension of life to every successful character, creating the basic human ambiguity in which we can see reflections of our sometimes secret selves. This same polarity also gives dramatic form to the more successful stories of Wells (and of other writers), finding expression in opposing characters that represent opposing patterns of response, as the little people in *The Food of the Gods* stand for aspects of selfish individualism and the giants stand for unselfish devotion to social or racial goals.

In the Days of the Comet, the last and the least successful of Wells' scientific romances,[141] is interesting not only because it shows another step in the evolution of his ideas of progress, but but also because it shows how essential his own psychological conflict is to the structure of the more successful romances. Here he deliberately reverses his earlier pessimistic statement that the cosmos is implacably hostile to progress. He makes it arbitrarily benevolent. "The swish of a comet's tail cools and cleanses the human atmosphere, and jealousy, and with it war and poverty, vanish from the world."[142] With this unpredictable freak of cosmic chance, he removes the human limits upon progress and ends all the dramas that embody them.

The novel is meant to be a parable of the transformation that individual men must make for the sake of progress. In a sense, it is also a confession of the change in Wells himself which has set him free to undertake his long evangelism for the cause of global progress. Yet this victory has a curiously ironic aftermath, because the resulting tract for progress is an artistic failure.

Wells has come to feel that individual jealousy is the chief enemy of social progress; he believes that civilization has developed "by buying off or generalizing, socializing and legalizing jealousy and possessiveness, in sex as in property."[143] The story is plotted to show how the world would be changed by the removal of jealousy; the comet is simply a device invented for that purpose, and much of the action is equally didactic.

Although the setting is in a cluster of pottery towns, the narrator, Willie Leadford, is clearly the young Wells himself—or rather the jealous aspect of Wells, with the same religious and social and sexual conflicts that he reports in the autobiography, but without all the charm and complexity and social adaptability that made the living Wells so readily and variously successful. He is by no means the Wells described by Geoffrey West, "a friendly, likeable, lively boy, always ready for a 'lark,'"[144] or by his own

brother Frank as "a healthy and masterful child from the first." [145]
Willie's worn, devoted drudge of a mother is a bit of Wells' own
mother, secretly grieving for his dead infant sister. Nettie Stuart,
the distant cousin Willie loves, is very much like the cousin,
Isabel Mary Wells, who became Wells' own first wife. Willie's
savage jealousy is the same emotion Wells felt for Isabel.[146]

Yet, though the originals may be real, the characters are not.
The conflict that had been the living heart has been cut out.
Before the coming of the comet, Willie is the pure type of selfish
jealousy, his misery almost unrelieved by successful social
adjustments. After the passing of the comet, his new altruism is
equally pure, robbed of all the ambiguities that would make it a
really human trait. The two sides of his nature are never allowed
to come into real dramatic conflict, because the miracle of the
cometary gas intervenes like a *deus ex machina*. The ending, as
Wells admitted, is as far from reality as the Kingdom of Heaven.[147]

Penniless and in love, Willie suffers from jealousy of both
property and sex. The background of poverty, labor strife, and war
is planned to show that his predicament is universal. His Nettie
elopes with the rich widow's son. Maddened by jealousy, Willie
is hunting them down with a revolver when all their difficulties
vanish in the true light of the comet. This new illumination reveals to Willie what has been wrong with the world. As he tells
Nettie,

> These bodies of ours are not the bodies of angels. . . . In our
> bodies you can find evidence of the lowliest ancestry . . . some-
> thing of the fish . . . and a hundred traces of the ape" (Bk. III,
> Ch. 1, Sec. 4).

Jealousy is an atavistic monster, snarling in the path of progress
When it is removed, the millenium dawns at once.

These last of the early romances show a crucial step in the
evolution of Wells' ideas. As an individual, he has been in rebellion since his birth against all the formal institutions of society.
What he discovers in these romances is the paradox that the true
goals of the individual and society are the same. As the pam-
phleteer of progress, he is still attacking the old enemies of his
rebel individualism: the fossil social structures of religion and
convention and law that are the remains of dead progress in the
past. But he has found a new and cleansing motive for the attack:
he is fighting now for racial progress as a better means of individual satisfaction.

Even in these first tracts for progress, however, Wells is
expressing no blindly optimistic belief in natural law working to

advance human happiness. Rather, his most rosy expectations are always restrained by a realistic knowledge of the processes of nature and of the faults of men. He is never the voice of Victorian optimism, numerous critics to the contrary.[148] Even the optimistic vision of a perfect future in *In the Days of the Comet* is subject to a pessimistic reading, for the people of the story are so hopelessly mired in jealousy that nothing less than the miraculous comet could have set them free. Nor was even their freedom welcome to Wells' Victorian readers, who were scandalized by the notion of love without jealousy.[149]

Our survey of the early fiction in the following chapters will show that Wells' ideas of progress were controlled from the beginning by his vision of mankind at the mercy of a chaotic and uncaring cosmos, by his sense of the painfully refractory stuff of human nature, and by his ironic awareness that even the most successful evolutionary adaptations of the future world are unlikely to base themselves upon the dreams of progressive liberalism.

The Limits of Progress:

Cosmic

1   Defining the Limits

"It is surely significant," writes Norman Nicholson,

> that the man who preached progress more eloquently than anyone
> else should be the one who had the most vivid vision of cosmic
> accident, and who realized . . . that the destiny of the whole
> earth . . . hangs by a thread.[1]

The significance is that Wells preached progress not out of confident hope, but out of cold desperation. Uniquely gifted both with the analytic brain that might have served a great scientist and with the creative imagination of a great artist, he saw the probable shape of the future more vividly, by the testimony of his work, than any other man of his time. Distressed by his own visions of the world to come, he strove for many years to change it, with dramatic warnings, impatient exhortations, and attempts at mass education. As Nicholson says,

> Wells was aware from the first that the development of scientific
> knowledge was not in itself any guarantee of progress, and many
> of his romances were based on the idea that science, divorced
> from humanity, . . . may bring disaster to mankind.[2]

But we exist in double jeopardy, from within ourselves and from without. Though the deadliest danger may be our own

47

heritage, we also inhabit a hostile cosmos. Lecturing in 1902, Wells reviewed a whole series of possible external perils. He speculated that some great unsuspected mass of matter might swirl out of space and destroy all life upon earth. He suggested that some unknown disease might end the human race, "some trailing cometary poison, some great emanation of vapor from the interior of the earth." He warned that "there may arise new animals to prey upon us by land and sea, and there may come some drug or wrecking madness into the minds of men." He considered the "reasonable certainty" that the solar system will continue to run down "until some day this earth of ours, tideless and slow moving, will be dead and frozen and all that has lived upon it will be frozen out and done with."[3]

In *The Discovery of the Future*, he writes that

> I do not believe in these things, because I have come to believe
> in certain other things, in the coherence and purpose in the world
> and in the greatness of human destiny.[4]

Earlier, however, during the last years of the century, the years of doubt and discovery which produced the best of the scientific romances and most of the short stories, he was still very much aware of the cosmic indifference to our survival. His studies of science, especially of biology, had given him a view of the probable future that he could neither accept nor ignore. Such thinkers as Malthus had led him to look at humanity in the emotionless light of biology. "Probably no more shattering book than the *Essay on Population* has ever been written, or ever will be written," he comments in *Anticipations*.[5]

> It was aimed at the facile liberalism of the deists and the atheists
> of the eighteenth century; it made clear as daylight that all forms
> of social reconstruction, all dreams of earthly golden ages, must
> be either futile or insincere or both, until the problems of human
> increase were manfully faced. . . . It aimed simply to wither the
> rationalistic utopias of the time, and, by anticipation, all the
> communisms, socialisms, and earthly paradise movements that
> have since been so abundantly audible in the world.

The writer of those words was hardly a preacher of inevitable and automatic progress! The earlier Wells, as his fiction shows, seems rather to have been fascinated with his imaginative exploration of the darkest aspects of the cosmos. At the very beginning of his writing career, as Anthony West observes, he had broken with Herbert Spencer's sort of progressive optimism. In "The Rediscovery of the Unique,"[6] he rejects the whole idea of evolutionary progress, "which depends on a picture of the universe in

which mind is increasingly valuable.''[7] He accepts in its stead
the mechanistic view that the world is ''nothing but a mere heap
of dust, fortuitously agitated.'' West comments that

it is impossible to be an optimist believing in inevitable progress
if you also believe in a universe in which mind figures only as a
local accident. There is also considerable difficulty in reconciling
the idea of progress with a universe which by its essential nature
cannot support a permanent world order. That Wells should have
dealt with the ideological basis of pessimism in his first serious
piece of writing throws some light on the real cast of his mind.

The prominence of the idea of progress in the early fiction
does not mean that Wells was writing tracts for it or against it.
The tracts came later. His major aim, during those beginning
years, was more probably to find himself as a creative writer, to
discover and perfect his own means of expression. He writes in
Experiment in Autobiography that in the years 1893-1894, under
the influence of his friend Walter Low, ''I was beginning to write
again in any scraps of time I could snatch from direct money-
earning. I was resuming my criticism of life.''[8] The life that he
criticized most searchingly, it would seem, was his own. The
autobiography, as well as the fiction, reveals the clash of discordant attitudes and emotions in his mind. He was his mother's
son, no less than his father's. He had learned contempt for a
useless aristocracy, but he had also been taught to fear the raw
proletariat. He had trained his mind to the disciplines of science,
but he had forgotten neither the traditional culture nor the desperate emotions of his youth. He hoped for a better world, but his
idealism clashed with a bitter knowledge of real human life.

The idea of progress in his early work may best be regarded
as a metaphor, perhaps, around which he was striving to organize
all these discrepant attitudes and emotions. The early science
fiction may be examined as a laboratory in which Wells was seeking to find and test his own attitudes. A study of the fiction from
this viewpoint will clarify the processes by which the tension
between unreconciled attitudes gives life and form; it will often
reveal the sources of the validity and intensity and depth evident
in the early fiction but lacking from much of what Wells wrote
after this tension had begun to subside.

As biologist, Wells sees us as only one more species swept
along by the flow of evolution, commonly blind to our nature and
our future. As human being, he longs to help us discover and guide
our destiny, but he finds small room for hope that intelligence can
free us from the cosmic laws and control all life. His early fiction

often dramatizes this conflict of hope and fear for the future of man. His troubled emotions clothe themselves in troubled characters; even the details of setting are frequently revealing.

Weather phenomena symbolize the hostile or indifferent nature of the cosmos. A hailstorm greets the Time Traveller with a symbolic chill when he arrives in the future world where even the elements seem generally to have been tamed (Ch. 3), and an icy wind and showering snowflakes in the more remote future warn him of the nearing death of the planet (Ch. 11). The Martians, in *The War of the Worlds*, have been spurred to their high progress by "the secular cooling" of Mars (Bk. I, Ch. 1), and the narrator himself, at the peak of his suffering under the Martians, is beaten with "a thin hail." In *When the Sleeper Wakes*, the snow on the city roofs is in symbolic contrast with the sheltered warmth within, showing the human victory over the cosmos to be narrow or illusory (Ch. 8). In *First Men in the Moon*, the freezing atmosphere represents the stern cosmic forces which have driven the Selenites to their ultimate degree of evolutionary adaptation, and which now menace Bedford himself (Ch. 18).

The early science fiction is first of all good fiction, the characters engaging and the invention bright and the narrative absorbing. Beneath the surface story, however, the main thematic emphasis is on the hazards to continued human progress: on the cosmic limits that promise to cut it short, on the human flaws that threaten to spoil it. Even when Wells admits the occasional short-term success of adaptive change, his evaluation of its fruits is seldom enthusiastic. In this chapter and those following, we shall consider in some detail first his imaginative exploration of the cosmic limits, next his study of the human limits, and finally his usually pessimistic evaluations of progress achieved.

Any separation of the novels and stories into such categories is, of course, arbitrary. The scheme is imposed upon the fiction, not discovered in it. At this point in his career, Wells was not writing a thesis on progress; he was striving instead to give objective form and aesthetic distance to some of the gravest conflicts within his own personality. The idea of progress is simply one important metaphor. He does not set out to discuss first the external and then the internal limits upon progress and then to examine the consequences of progress beyond these limits. Often, in a single story, he does all these things. *The Time Machine*, for example, concludes with a dramatic emphasis upon the cosmic limits, when the vividly realized collapse of the solar system precludes further progress. But there is an earlier emphasis upon the human limits, when the human race is shown differentiating into the dainty cattle of the upper world and the gray troglodytes that eat them. There is also a sardonic evaluation of the consequences of progress, in the revelation that normal evolutionary adaptation has produced these two new breeds of not-quite men. Here, however, *The Time Machine* will be classified as dealing with the external or cosmic limits. *The War of the Worlds*, in which human survival is threatened by invasion from Mars, seems logically to belong in the same group. So do a number of the short stories which deal with astronomical or biological hazards to the indefinite advancement of mankind.

2 The Time Machine

If the early fiction of Wells owes its form and life to the tension between incompatible attitudes, the nature of that inner conflict is easiest to see, perhaps, in *The Time Machine*,[9] his first major work and perhaps his most brilliant. Though much of his later writing was done hastily and inadequately revised, he labored painstakingly through at least seven versions of *The Time Machine*, of which five survive.[10] The earliest is the unfinished serial, "The Chronic Argonauts," published in the *Science Schools Journal*—of which Wells himself had been a founder and the first editor—for April, May, and June, 1888. By 1892, Wells had made two revisions of the story. Though these have been lost, Wells read parts of them to a college friend, A. Morley Davies, whose description is quoted by Geoffrey West.[11] The fourth version consists of seven unsigned articles published in the *National Observer* between March and June, 1894, while W. E. Henley was editor; this series has no sustained narrative, and it was broken off when Henley left the *Observer*. When he became editor of the *New Review*, he accepted a narrative version and ran it in five parts, January through May, 1895. Two differing book versions were published the same year, by Heinemann in London and Holt in New York. All these careful revisions show that Wells, in the beginning, was a literary artist almost as conscientious as Henry James.

Comparing the first attempt with the finished novel, we can clearly see Wells' conflicting attitudes giving form and dramatic life to his materials. "The Chronic Argonauts" is melodramatic, wordy, derivative, and conventional. Wells himself wrote of it in the autobiography:

The prose was over-elaborate. . . . And the story is clumsily

invented, and loaded with irrelevant sham significance. The time
traveller, for example, is called Nebo-gipfel, though manifestly
Mount Nebo had no business whatever in the story. There was no
Promised Land ahead.[12]

A striking difference between the first version and the finished
novel is in the treatment of the idea of progress. "The Chronic
Argonauts" merely hints at the idea. A few symbols of progress
do appear, in the name Nebogipfel, in the invention and explanation of the time machine, in the statement that it has been used
to secure "valuable medical, social, and physiographical data
for all time."[13] We never learn, however, exactly what those data
are. The symbols of progress are completely submerged beneath
contrasting metaphors of decay, terror, and death. A figure of
fear, not of hope, Nebogipfel is the scientist as destroyer. The
most vividly presented part of the setting is a decaying Manse
where foul murder has been done. The action, so far as it goes
in the three installments Wells wrote, is conventional gothic
melodrama with overtones of "unearthly noises and inexplicable
phenomena."[14] Instead of the people of the future, Wells introduces a mob of degenerate Welsh villagers.

"A cleansing course of Swift and Sterne intervened before the
idea was written again for Henley's National Observer," as Wells
confesses in his preface to the Atlantic Edition.[15] The final version takes its shape from Wells' intention to explore the possible
future history of mankind. The satanic scientist and the haunted
Manse and the angry villagers are gone. The new Time Traveller
is an amiable and rather ordinary man, who explains his extra-
ordinary machine to a group of completely ordinary skeptics in a
setting of commonplace detail carefully selected to contrast with
the wonder of travel in time. The time machine itself is made real
by means of a convincing laboratory demonstration which is followed by ingeniously created and vividly given sense impressions
of the actual flight through time, with night following day "like
the flapping of a black wing," and the trees on the hillside
"growing and changing like puffs of vapor, now brown, now green"
(Ch. 3). Since Wells was an ardent cyclist at the time he wrote,
he borrowed sensations and experiences from his familiar sport.
The time machine itself is apparently very much like a bicycle;
it turns over and stuns the Time Traveller when he stops too
suddenly in the year 802,701 A.D.

The chief plot interest of the middle section of the novel
comes from the effort of the Time Traveller to learn the real
nature of his future world, to trace out the results of eight hundred

thousand years of change. Enormous but crumbling buildings around him are evidence both of long progress and of subsequent decay. Tiny, childlike men and women flock around him: they are the Eloi, idle vegetarians whose lives of aimless play are passed in weedless parks and great communal halls. The time machine is stolen; in attempting to recover it he discovers an underground world of vast mysterious machines and finds that the Eloi are fed and cared for by a race of hideous albino creatures like small apes. At length he understands that the parasitic Eloi are descendents of the Victorian upper classes, and that the little underground apes, the Morlocks, are the children of the proletariat. Now the masters, the Morlocks breed the Eloi for food.

Escaping on the recovered time machine into the infinite future, he finds mankind extinct and the solar system itself near death, the earth spiraling inward toward the dying sun. Yet life persists: bright green moss grows on the sunward faces of the rocks, and enormous crab-like things crawl along the shore of an oily, tideless sea. The Time Traveller is appalled by

> the red eastern sky, the northward blackness, the salt Dead Sea, the stony beach crawling with these foul, slow-stirring monsters, the uniform poisonous-looking green of the lichenous plants, the thin air that hurts one's lungs (Ch. 11).

Attacked by the gigantic crabs, he ventures even further into the future, testing an ultimate frontier of possible progress. An icy night falls, as the red sun is eclipsed. Ill and shivering, he sees a moving creature.

> It was a round thing . . . black against the weltering blood-red water, and it was hopping fitfully about. . . . A terrible dread of lying helpless in that remote and awful twilight sustained me while I clambered upon the saddle (Ch. 11).

So, from this vision of a time when the last chance of progress on earth has ended in "abominable desolation," the Time Traveller returns to the nineteenth century.

Some few flaws from the earlier drafts are left in this final version of the novel, but Wells has generally been able to redeem them with his emerging narrative genius. The story of Weena, the little Eloi girl who falls in love with the Time Traveller after he has saved her from drowning, is an unconvincing vestige of Victorian sentimental romance. The entire plot is manipulated to add dramatic interest to the imaginative tour of the future which is Wells' main concern. Sometimes this manipulation has awkward results, especially in the double climax of the escape from the

Morlocks and the vision of the end of the world, and in the improbable readiness of the exhausted Time Traveller to talk for most of the night after his return. The ending, in which he does not come back from a second expedition, is a purely arbitrary device, implying little of either theme or character. But for the reader under the spell of Wells' paradoxical ideas, prophetic speculations, and persuasive narrative magic, such faults scarcely matter.

In this first and most sweeping survey of our imagined future, Wells evaluates the idea of progress from many angles. The human limits upon progress appear most strikingly in the conservative guests who greet the Time Traveller's discoveries with varied attitudes of stupidity, bewilderment, and doubt. "It sounds plausible enough tonight," says the Medical Man. "But wait until tomorrow. Wait for the common sense of the morning" (Ch. 1). The future world is filled with evidence of long progressive ages: the magnificent buildings and surviving works of art, the elimination of weeds and insects and germs of disease, the apparently complete subjugation of nature. Yet the Time Traveller not only finds that this age-long march of progress has been in vain; he finds that it has been in fact the cause of the later decay. This law of nature, that progress itself results in degeneration, is a cosmic limit that shapes the body of the novel. A second cosmic limit, which shapes the concluding section and provides the second climax, appears in the final collapse of the solar system, the planets falling one by one into the dying sun.

This particular catastrophe, incidentally, no longer seems so near as it did when Wells was writing. The accepted theories of his day held that the sun's energy, being chiefly gravitational, could last only a few million years. More recent theories, offering atomic sources for solar energy, have extended the probable life of the solar system a thousand times. In spite of such sweeping revisions, however, the physical limits upon human progress seem as implacable now as they did to Wells. In the new light of the exploding atom, human life looks no more secure.

The other limit, the law that progress sets its own bounds, is worth a closer look. Wells, at least in the early fiction, is no utopian setting up an ideal world as the goal of all progress. A scientist instead, he sees the world as a dynamic train of cause and effect. Progress, conceivably, may lead to some sort of perfection, but even perfection in turn must result in something else. "What," the Time Traveller asks, "is the cause of human intelligence and vigor?" He answers himself: "Hardship and freedom:

conditions under which the active, strong, and subtle survive and the weaker go to the wall.'' He points out that

> physical courage and the love of battle . . . are no great help—may even be hindrances—to a civilised man. And in a state of physical balance and security, power, intellectual as well as physical, would be out of place (Ch. 4).

The Time Traveller grieves for the suicide of the human intellect.

> It had set itself steadfastly toward comfort and ease, a balanced society with security and permanency as its watchword, it had attained its hopes—to come to this at last. . . . There is no intelligence where there is no change and no need of change (Ch. 10).

Thus the Time Traveller discovers that progress limits itself. This fact he sees as natural law, an aspect of the cosmos as deadly to the dream of unlimited perfection as are the physical laws of mass and energy that decree the death of planets.

The Time Machine, in summary, is a profoundly pessimistic assessment of progress. Anthony West has stressed its gloomy theme. The machine carries the Time Traveller to a point in the future

> from which it is obvious that a cosmic event is impending which will destroy the whole frame of reference in which mind, consciousness and experience have any meaning. . . . Wells is saying that the universe, like Kali, gives birth only to destroy, and that the scientific apparatus for examining reality can only bring home to man that everything he can do, think, or feel is finally futile. The end for the environment, as for the race and the individual, is extinction.[16]

The Time Traveller himself holds no brief for progress. In the epilogue, added for a later edition, the narrator says of him,

> He, I know—for the question had been discussed among us long before the Time Machine was made—thought but cheerlessly of the Advancement of Mankind, and saw in the growing pile of civilisation only a foolish heaping that must inevitably fall back upon and destroy its makers in the end.

3 The War of the Worlds

The War of the Worlds[17] takes its shape from another aspect of the cosmic limits upon progress, one merely hinted at in *The Time Machine*. In the major climax of *The Time Machine*, Wells shows the future of man eclipsed by the physical nature of the universe. In *The War of the Worlds* he explores a more immediate limit, one set by the laws of life. A biologist, Wells views mankind not as the completed achievement of creation, but simply as one species evolving in competition with others, adapting to the same environmental pressures, making the same hard fight for survival. In *The War of the Worlds*, as in a group of short stories written during the same early years, he shows mankind clashing with an alien biology.

The novel is constructed with a classic simplicity. The alien biology is introduced in the opening sentence, with this world "being watched keenly and closely by intelligences greater than man's and yet as mortal as his own" (Bk. I, Ch. 1). The Martians,

> minds that are to our minds as ours are to the beasts that perish, intellects vast and cool and unsympathetic, regarded this earth with envious eyes, and slowly and surely drew their plans against us.

Their planet is dying, and "the immediate pressure of necessity has brightened their intellects, enlarged their powers, and hardened their hearts." The invaders reach the earth in ten immense missiles, fired at intervals of twenty-four hours. Night after night, they fall near London. The Martians emerge to subjugate the earth. Men, curious and friendly at first, are stung into armed resistance by the unprovoked Martian attacks, and finally driven out of London in dazed and helpless panic. Although two or three Martians are killed, their superior weapons easily crush the best human defenses. Their victory seems secure—when suddenly they die, rotted by the micro-organisms of decay.

Telling his strange tale with immense gusto and skill, Wells avoids most of the defects that flaw *The Time Machine*. Fittingly, since men are such helpless victims of the cosmic struggle for survival, there is no human hero. The narrator is simply an observer of the action; writing after the war is over, he is able to fill out his account with scientific explanations, summaries of the wider action, and philosophic interpretation. Documentary in style, the narrative is so appallingly convincing that Orson Welles was able to create an actual panic in New Jersey on an October evening of 1938, with a radio version of it.[18] [19] The technique is Defoesque: precisely pictured fact is mixed with ingenious invention. The Martians are invented, but their targets are overwhelmingly convincing: the English countryside, the towns, the victims. In the autobiography, Wells has written how he "wheeled about the district marking down suitable places and people for destruction."[20] The writing is economical and objective, the details tellingly selected.

> Then we crept out of the house, and ran as quickly as we could
> down the ill-made road by which I had come overnight. The houses
> seemed deserted. In the road lay a group of three charred bodies
> close together, struck dead by the Heat-Ray; and here and there
> were things that people had dropped—a clock, a slipper, a silver
> spoon (Bk. I, Ch. 12).

Now and then Wells trips over his impressionistic method of
using bits of trivial detail to cover vagueness in more important
matters. At one point he writes of the Black Smoke, a Martian
poison gas:

> Save that an unknown element giving a group of four lines in the
> blue of the spectrum is concerned, we are still entirely ignorant
> of the nature of this substance (Bk. I, Ch. 15).

Later he forgets the detail, but not the method. "Spectrum analysis of the black powder points unmistakably to the presence of an
unknown element with a brilliant group of three lines in the green"
(Bk. II, Ch. 10). Generally, however, he is far more successful;
one of the first comments, a long and favorable review in the
Spectator, compared the novel with Defoe's *Journal of the Plague
Year.*[21] The story as a whole creates an unforgettable impression
of reality; the descriptions of devastation and panic might almost
have been based upon actual observation of twentieth-century
war.

Traces of the Victorian sentimental romance appear in a few
chapters about the narrator's younger brother, a medical student
in London, who rescues a conventional romantic heroine from
robbers and sees her and her companion safely through the invasion and across the channel to France. But even these chapters
are written in an objective style, with the emphasis not upon the
love story but upon the convincing particulars that suggest the
disintegration of a great city.

> It was a stampede—a stampede gigantic and terrible—without order
> and without goal, six million people, unarmed and unprovisioned,
> driving headlong. It was the beginning of the rout of civilisation,
> of the massacre of mankind (Bk. I, Ch. 17).

The ending of the story, at first glance a flaw, is actually a
tellingly ironic restatement of the main theme. The ending does
violate the dramatic rule that the central plot problem must be
solved by the action or the nature of the protagonist, with no
interference from coincidence. The germs that kill the Martians
appear at first glimpse to be coincidental, simply a convenient
deus ex machina invented by the author to bring about a pleasing
conclusion. A second glance, however, shows this solution

arising logically from the theme that progress is controlled by biological laws—which bind Martians, no less than men. Meeting a competing species of life against which they have no biological defenses, the Martians are eliminated. Ironically, their lack of defenses is probably the result of their own past progress. "Micro-organisms . . . have either never appeared upon Mars or Martian sanitary science eliminated them ages ago" (Bk. II, Ch. 2). Again, as in *The Time Machine*, Wells shows the culmination of progress leading to decline.

The War of the Worlds, like *The Time Machine*, draws its vital dramatic tension from the clash of Wells' own contradictory attitudes toward progress. The novel is artistically successful because Wells has found effective metaphors and has placed them in a plot which reveals their meaning through dramatic action. The Martians stand for progress, continued almost to infinity. The human characters represent attitudes toward progress which range from blind ignorance to insane terror. Risking the error of identifying Wells' own attitudes with those of his characters, and allowing for the fact that in plot construction the need for powerful antagonistic forces can betray the uncommitted writer into a sort of accidental pessimism, we can hardly avoid feeling that the early Wells regards the future with a fascinated dread. He seems to relish contemplating "the extinction of man";[22] in the midst of *The War of the Worlds*, he writes Elizabeth Healey,

> I'm doing the dearest little serial for Pearson's new magazine, in which I completely wreck and destroy Woking—killing my neighbors in painful and eccentric ways—then proceed via Kingston and Richmond to London, which I sack, selecting South Kensington for feats of peculiar atrocity.[23]

A scientist, Wells knows that adaptive change is inevitable; he has even developed a rational technique for studying the shape of things to come.[24] A humanist, he loves the values of the past and the people he knows. He is appalled by the future he foresees—yet he lingers almost lovingly over each new figure of terror and death.

Such ambivalent attitudes shape the novel in many ways. In the body of the story, the suspense is intensified by hints of human decline. Writing from his viewpoint in the time after the end of the war, the narrator implies that progress has been reversed. Recalling the white cloth and the silver and glass on his dining table at home, he comments that "in those days even philosophical writers had many little luxuries" (Bk. I, Ch. 7). At the end of the novel, however, there has been no apparent harm inflicted on earth outside a small area of England; even the greater part of London has escaped. A study of the derelict Martian machines has given "an enormous impetus to terrestial invention" (Bk. II, Ch. 2).

The narrator—the "philosophical writer"—is unusual among the human characters in that he accepts the fact of progress. Looking back at the days of peace and plenty before the Martian invasion, he writes, "For my own part, I was much occupied in learning to ride the bicycle, and busy upon a series of papers discussing the probable development of moral ideas as civilisation progressed" (Bk. I, Ch. 1). At the end of the stories he returns to his unfinished papers with a changed attitude. He writes that

> our views of the human future must be greatly modified by these events. We have learned now that we cannot regard this planet as being fenced in and a secure abiding-place for Man; we can never anticipate the unseen good or evil that may come upon us suddenly out of space (Bk. II, Ch. 10).

Yet his progressive optimism is not entirely gone; he suggests that men may later reach new planets too.

> Dim and wonderful is the vision I have conjured up in my mind of life spreading slowly from this little seed-bed of the solar system throughout the inanimate vastness of siderial space. But that is a remote dream. It may be, on the other hand, that the destruction of the Martians is only a reprieve. To them, and not to us, perhaps, is the future ordained (Bk. II, Ch. 10).

The pitiless Martian onslaught has convinced the narrator that progress does not increase goodness. Despite the fitful gleams of optimism with which he relieves the ending of the story, he writes that "I must confess the stress and danger of the time have left an abiding sense of doubt and insecurity in my mind." Dark visions haunt him.

> Of a night I see the black powder darkening the silent streets, and the contorted bodies shrouded in that layer; they rise upon me tattered and dog-bitten . . . mad distortions of humanity (Bk. II, Ch. 10).

Two minor characters, the curate and the artilleryman, represent two opposed attitudes toward progress, neither of which Wells himself seems to admire. The narrator, emerging from the scalding water into which he has dived to escape the Heat-Ray, becomes aware of the curate as "a seated figure in soot-smudged shirt-sleeves," inquiring, "Why are these things permitted? What sins have we done?'' (Bk. I, Ch. 13.) When the Martians struck, the curate had been walking after the morning service to clear his brain; dazed, now, he cannot accept the fact of change. The narrator soon learns to hate his "trick of helpless exclamation, his stupid rigidity of mind" (Bk. II, Ch. 3). When the two men are trapped in a ruined house from which they can watch the Martians emerging from their missile, the curate slowly breaks under the pressure of terror. When he will not keep silent, the narrator kills him. His body is dragged away by the Martians that his raving has alarmed. His inflexible resistance to change, the attitude of conventional religion, has led only to death.

If the curate can be taken to symbolize the traditional culture with its pessimistic resistance to progress, the artilleryman seems to stand for the optimistic and progressive culture of the technologist. He lacks traditional education, but he shows a surprising talent for survival. A practical man, he is quick to accept and take advantage of the changes in his environment. He is immediately prepared to fight for survival in a world where

> there won't be any more blessed concerts for a million years or so; there won't be any Royal Academy of Arts, and no nice little feeds at restaurants (Bk. II, Ch. 7).

Shrewdly, he has turned back from the fugitive mobs, to seek his food and shelter under the feet of the Martians. A cosmic pessimist in his own right, he observes that

> it's just men and ants. There's the ants builds their cities, live their lives, have wars, revolutions, until the men want them out of the way, and then they go out of the way. That's what we are now—just ants.

And, he adds, "We're eatable ants." Under the new order of things, "Cities, nations, civilisation, progress—that's all over. That game's up. We're beat."

Yet, with something of the desperate optimism of the later Wells himself, the artilleryman is laying plans for survival—even for continued human progress. Scornfully, he condemns the fearful, conformist majority of mankind.

> They'll come and be caught cheerful. They'll be quite glad after a bit. They'll wonder what people did before there were Martians to take care of them (Bk. II, Ch. 7).

Declaring that "we have to invent a sort of life where man can live and breed, and be sufficiently secure to bring the children up," he outlines a bold scheme for survival underground, in drains and subways and tunnels. He has even begun digging. When the narrator joins him, however, he proves to be easily distracted from his vast progressive schemes, by the temptations of looted food and drink and cigars and cards. Disillusioned, the narrator resolves "to leave this strange undisciplined dreamer of great things to his drink and gluttony, and go on into London." Thus, finally, the artilleryman becomes no more than a satiric thrust at the optimist planners of progress. The technological is no better than the traditional culture.

Although such symbolic figures sometimes debate Wells' quarrel with himself, his own attitudes toward progress appear more strikingly in his treatment of the invaders. For the Martians are not merely an alien species competing with men for control of the earth. Symbolically, they are also a final stage in the evolution of mankind. However sleepless, sexless, and monstrous they may be, the Martians are perhaps "descended from beings not unlike ourselves, by a gradual development of brain and hands" (Bk. II, Ch. 2). The narrator mentions "a certain speculative writer of quasi-scientific repute, writing long before the Martian invasion," who "forecast for man a final structure not unlike the actual Martian condition." This writer was Wells himself.[25] Attempting to forecast the tendency of natural selection, he had suggested that machines and chemical devices would gradually replace most of the parts and functions of the human body.

But the fact that Wells the scientist foresaw such evolutionary adaptations of mankind does not mean that Wells the human being approved them. Quite the contrary: he presents the Martians as vampire-like figures of horror. The first one emerging from the missile is "a big greyish rounded bulk, the size, perhaps, of a bear," glistening "like wet leather" (Bk. I, Ch. 4). The narrator, even before he sees the Martians feeding themselves by injecting human blood directly into their veins, is "overcome with disgust and dread" by the

> peculiar V-shaped mouth with its pointed upper lip . . . the incessant quivering of this mouth, the Gorgon groups of tentacles . . . the extraordinary intensity of the immense eyes . . . vital, intense, inhuman, crippled and monstrous . . . something fungoid in the oily brown skin, something in the clumsy deliberation of the tedious movements unspeakably nasty (Bk. I, Ch. 4).

If the Martians represent an ultimate projection of the consequences of human progress, all the benign possibilities are ignored. Wells, instead, places his heaviest emphasis on improvements in the art of war. Writing at Woking in 1896, he was able to outline future military developments in remarkable detail. His Martians, in their armored vehicles, advance against mankind with the panzer tactics of World War II. Their Black Smoke is a poison gas, dispersed in cannisters fired from rockets, and they are developing military aircraft for use in the heavier air of earth. They are waging total war. The scenes of destruction by the Heat-Ray suggest Hiroshima, and the chapter in which the refugees from the vicinity of London are ferried across the Channel to France by "the most amazing crowd of shipping of all sorts that it is possible to imagine" (Bk. I, Ch. 17) reminds one of Dunkerque.

Finally, it is the great past progress of the Martians, rather than any act of their intended human victims, that leads to their destruction. Having lost their immunity to the germs of decay, they are "overtaken by a death that must have seemed as incomprehensible to them as any death could be" (Bk. II, Ch. 8). As painfully as mankind, they have encountered the cosmic limits upon progress. The ultimate creation of evolutionary adaptation has been eliminated by the simplest. Progress, following cosmic law, has limited itself.

4 "The Star" and Other Stories

Wells' short stories, more numerous and varied than the novels, offer an even wider insight into the conflicts symbolized by his resistance to the idea of progress. Nearly all written during the first seven or eight years of his success, while he was still the literary artist, they brought good prices from magazines; in 1901 he told Arnold Bennett that the *Strand* was paying him £125 a story.[26] They were collected in a series of volumes: *The Stolen Bacillus and Other Incidents* (1895), *The Plattner Story and Others* (1897), *Tales of Space and Time* (1899), and *Twelve Stories and a Dream* (1903). Later, a selection from these volumes appeared with a few additional stories in *The Country of the Blind and Other Stories* (1911). A final collection, *The Short Stories of H. G. Wells,*[27] includes all the stories in the earlier volumes and two or three newer ones. Only a few other bits of short fiction, such as *The Croquet Player*,[28] were published later.

The thick single volume of Wells' collected short stories is still a delight to read, rich in ideas and humor and surprise, full of an unquenchable cheerful vitality. The short stories, like the longer romances, are refreshingly free of the hero-and-villain and boy-gets-girl formulas of magazine fiction. Never a systematic thinker, neither was Wells a systematic writer. Though he often tried to set up a regular working routine, such efforts always collapsed. He told an interviewer in 1906 that he could do more in an hour of "impulse than in a whole week of regular effort." [29] Early in his career,

> it was his custom to get up in the morning and talk with Mrs. Wells about any ideas he had in his head, and after breakfast he would sit down to work them out. If the inspiration did not come then he pushed the matter aside because it was sure to come later. [30]

In this undisciplined way, he was able to write two or three articles or stories a week; and such romances as *The War of the Worlds* and *The Invisible Man* were also written

> in intermittent periods of spontaneousness. They were often dropped in the midst of other work, then toiled at, taken to pieces, and put together in all sorts of ways.

As he wrote Arnold Bennett:

> The Imagination moves in a mysterious way its wonders to perform. I can assure you that I am *not* doing anything long and weird and strong in the vein of *The Time Machine* and I never intend to. I would as soon take hat and stick and start out into the street to begin a passionate love. If it comes—well and good. [31]

Much of the freshness and charm of all the early fiction comes from this free creativity. Later, when Wells tries to chop characters and plot to fit a didactic scheme, as he does in *In the Days of the Comet*, the result is artistic disaster. [32] Not only was Wells impatient with fiction formulas, but also with the short story form itself. He commented in a letter to his father in 1898:

> I'm also under contract to do a series of stories for the *Strand Magazine* but I don't like the job. . . . If you send them anything a bit novel they are afraid their readers won't understand. [33]

When the spontaneous inspirations ceased to come, a few years later, he did not resort to formulas; he simply stopped writing short stories. [34]

Although there is a pattern in most of the early fiction, it is remarkably flexible. In Wells' own words, it is

> the method of bringing some fantastically possible or impossible thing into a commonplace group of people, and working out their reactions with the greatest gravity and reasonableness. [35]

Once he has arranged for the familiar to confront the unknown, he leaves the outcome to the forces of character and situation,

without the intrusion of sentimentality. As he wrote in an introduction, "I would discover I was peering into remote and mysterious worlds ruled by an order logical indeed but other than our
common sanity."[36]

More often comic than grim, the short stories have none of the
sugary optimism of much Victorian popular fiction. Wells has no
bias for things as they are. Rather, he is seeking to disturb his
readers with

> the vivid realisation of some disregarded possibility in such a way
> as to comment on the false securities and fatuous self-satisfaction
> of everyday life.[37]

Forecasting "The Extinction of Man" in his essay of that title,
he cheerfully remarks that "in no case does the record of the
fossils show a really dominant species succeeded by its own
descendents."[38] Serenely absorbed in the downfall of man, he
considers several of the potential rivals that later appear in his
fiction: the gigantic crabs of *The Time Machine*, the conqueror
ants of "The Empire of the Ants," the oceanic monsters of "The
Sea Raiders," and the deadly bacteria of *The War of the Worlds*.

Their spontaneity makes the early stories a valid record of
psychological conflict. Though most of the stories "are just
stories, pure and simple, things written with amusement to
amuse,"[39] they are full of Wells' irreverence for convention and
tradition. His general plot pattern, conflict between the familiar
and the new, leads naturally to comment on progress; of more
than sixty stories, perhaps three out of four use the metaphor of
progress, though not in any consistent way. A few such stories
as "The Land Ironclads"[40] look approvingly at progress. Others,
for example "Jimmy Goggles the God"[41] and "The New Accelerator,"[42] exploit some aspect of change chiefly for the sake of
comedy or surprise. Generally, however, the short stories, like
the romances, reveal profound misgivings about the limits, the
direction, and the consequences of the future evolution of mankind.

The cosmic insignificance of man is the theme of the remarkable vision of the universe, "Under the Knife."[43] The narrator,
already detached by long illness from all the emotions of life,
undergoes a surgical operation. Dying, as he believes, under the
surgeon's knife, he finds himself outside his body. The doctors
and the operating room and the earth itself swirl away, leaving
his detached mind adrift in space.

> Presently, when I looked again, the little earth seemed no bigger

> than the sun. . . . I swam motionless in vacancy, and, without a
> trace of terror or astonishment, watched the speck of cosmic dust
> we call the world fall away from me.[44]

His disembodied intelligence drifts through time as well as
space. The moon spins visibly around the earth, and then the
whole solar system is swept away from him. The stars and their
planets stream past him like dust in a sunbeam, and the entire
universe shrinks at last in cosmic darkness "to one minute disc
of hazy light."[45] This striking vision of the infinite smallness
of mankind against the cosmic scale of space and time is not
only grippingly real but astronomically correct. Seen against this
scale, the idea of human progress is reduced to the vanishing
point.

"The Star"[46] is a brief but richly imagined bit of future history constructed upon the pessimistic statement that the future
of mankind is utterly dependent upon the blindly random movement of unseen forces in a cosmos where the human race is no
more consequential than the germs upon a speck of dust. A dark
object wandering out of interstellar space collides with the planet
Neptune, and the resulting incandescent mass falls toward the
sun, just missing the earth. The resulting cataclysms are described with economy and power.

> Upon all the mountains of the earth the snow and ice began to melt
> that night, and all the rivers coming out of high country flowed
> thick and turbid, and soon—in their upper reaches—with swirling
> trees and the bodies of beasts and men.[47]

A tide fifty feet high drowns the lowland cities.

> The tangled summits of the Indian jungles were aflame in a thou-
> sand places, and below the hurrying waters around the stems were
> dark objects that still struggled feebly and reflected the blood-red
> tongues of fire.[48]

Pessimists conclude that human progress has ended, that "man
has lived in vain."[49] Millions perish, but the star passes. The
cosmic insignificance of mankind upon the cosmic scale is ironically stressed in the comment of a Martian astronomer upon the
extent of the damage to earth.

> All the familiar continental markings and the masses of the seas
> remain intact, and indeed the only difference seems to be a shrink-
> age of the white discoloration (supposed to be frozen water) round
> either pole.[50]

In "The Remarkable Case of Davidson's Eyes,"[51] Wells makes
a novel use of the same pessimistic theme: that human survival

is at the mercy of half-known and uncontrolled cosmic forces. Davidson, working at the Harlow Technical College, is bending with his head between the poles of a big electromagnet when lightning strikes the laboratory. His eyes are affected, so that he can see an island at the antipodes, though he is blind to things around him. (The ingenious theory of a "kink in space" with which Wells explains his peculiar accident has become a standard device in subsequent science fiction.) The magnet has twisted the retinal elements of Davidson's eyes through a fourth dimension. "Two points might be a yard away on a sheet of paper, and yet be brought together by bending the paper around."[52] Although Davidson suffers no permanent harm, the effect of the story comes chiefly from the sense of man at the mercy of the cosmic unknown. The peculiar power of these early stories arises from Wells' genius at making this unknown almost painfully near and real.

"Through a Window,"[53] although it has no direct reference to progress, is a melodramatic reminder that men survive or die at the whim of forces they can neither see nor control. Bailey, sitting in a room with both legs broken and set, entertains himself by looking through a window at the traffic upon the Thames. He remains an idly detached observer, secure from any personal commitment, until the day when a Malay seaman runs amuck, climbs through the window, and dies reaching for Bailey with his creese.

An exploration of our astronomical limits is interrupted in the story, "In the Avu Observatory,"[54] by an unexpected biological attack. The astronomer Woodhouse is at his telescope, "watching a little group of stars in the Milky Way," when a vast wing sweeps toward him out of the dark, a claw tears his cheek, and his ankle is "gripped and held by a row of keen teeth."[55] The unknown attacker escapes into the darkness over the jungle. As Woodhouse reports to the chief observer, who groans at the quotation, "There are more things in heaven and earth—and more particularly in the forests of Borneo—than are dreamt of in our philosophies."[56]

Perhaps because such biological limits offer more variety, complexity, and irony than do the equally severe astronomical limits of "The Star" and *The Time Machine*, Wells wrote many stories in which men are threatened or overshadowed by rival forms of life. In "The Crystal Egg,"[57] for example, the tragically bare existence of the hero is brought into stark perspective by a glimpse of Mars. The egg is a television link between the earth and Mars. Its remarkable nature has been discovered by Mr. Cave, an ineffectual little antique-dealer. Cruelly bullied by his wife and step-children, he finds in the crystal object a brief escape. Though the Martians in this story are mounting no war against the earth, the wonders of their world are significantly contrasted with the mean, tormented poverty of Mr. Cave's life. The beautiful, birdlike Martians appear more worthy of progress than do men.

Holroyd, the viewpoint character of "The Empire of the Ants," [58] encounters the progressive rivals of mankind nearer home. A Lancashire engineer, he is in Brazil on a new gunboat sent to fight a plague of ants. An innocent young man straight from England, "where Nature is hedged, ditched, and drained into the perfection of submission," [59] he has been confident of progress. "He had taken it for granted that a day would come when everywhere about the earth, plow and culture, light tramways, and good roads, and ordered security, would prevail." [60] On the Amazon, however, he discovers the cosmic inconsequence of man. The forest is interminable. Scattered ruins of buildings suggest that the real masters here are the puma, the jaguar, and the ants. In a few miles of the forest, Holroyd reflects

> there must be more ants than there are men in the whole world! . . . They had a language, they had an intelligence! . . . Suppose presently the ants began to store knowledge. . . . use weapons, form great empires, sustained a planned and organized war? [61]

As the gunboat ascends the river, that does happen. A sudden evolutionary jump brings the uncertain benefits of progress to the ants, whose gigantic leaders wear clothing and have tools or weapons "strapped about their bodies by bright white bands like white metal threads." [62] Reluctantly, fearful of being called to account for wasting ammunition, the Creole captain fires his big gun and then steams back down the river, leaving the ants undefeated. As the story ends, their empire is still expanding.

> So far their action has been a steady progressive settlement, involving the flight or slaughter of every human being in the new areas they invade. . . . Holroyd at least is firmly convinced that they will finally dispossess man over the whole of tropical South America. [63]

Many other stories repeat this pattern, in which the exotic element is an evolutionary rival of mankind. The plant kingdom in "The Flowering of the Strange Orchid," [64] evolves at least a symbolic threat to human progress. The ocean gives birth to progressive rival species, in "In the Abyss," [65] and "The Sea Raiders." [66] The spirit world provides a malevolent and dangerous competitor in "The Stolen Body." [67] The land produces another rival species in the enormous flying spiders of "The Valley of Spiders." [68]

Though the novels and short stories discussed in this chapter express various moods and intentions, all of them are at least partly shaped by Wells' painful awareness that men exist within implacable cosmic limits, and that the continued evolution of mankind may be interrupted by physical or biological events beyond human control.

The Limits of Progress:

Human

1 Man Against Himself

Turning from the cosmic to the human limits on progress, we must keep in mind that this distinction is entirely arbitrary, a convenience for discussion but not a fact of nature. If man is only another random atom in an infinite universe, significant only to himself, then everything human is also cosmic. Whatever illusions he may cultivate, man is still, in the words of Huxley, "as purely a part of the cosmic process, as the humblest weed."[1] The human limits, as we shall discuss them here, are simply those cosmic limits internal to men.

However wholly natural, man is yet divided against himself. The human animal, perfected through evolution for survival as a solitary individual, is forever at odds with the more recent social animal who survives with his group by means of such new adaptations as mutual solidarity and the division of labor. This two-fold and conflicting nature of man, explained and documented by the facts of evolution, gave the early Wells his most significant literary material. For he, like other men, was at war with himself.[2]

This universal conflict between the two natures of man is, of course, no recent discovery. It underlies the symbolism of religion. It creates the problems of psychiatry and the law. Regarded with a sentimental self-pity, it becomes "the human condition."

It is the stuff of drama: tragedy and comedy differ simply in viewpoint. Tragedy identifies the observer with the suffering hero—the proud Oedipus, the jealous Othello, the aspiring Faust—who is doomed by the excess of primitive individualism that keeps him from adapting to the rule of the group. Comedy, on the other hand, identifies the observer with society, inviting not pity and terror inspired by the cosmic destruction visited upon the individual who refuses his duty to the race, but rather the laughter at some social type of failure to conform. When the social offender is allowed to become an individual with whom the observer can identify—as does Wells' Invisible Man, near the end of the novel—the effect veers promptly from comedy to tragedy. Though this human conflict is at the heart of much literature—one main function of literature is simply to transmit required patterns of response—it assumes a peculiar relevance to the study of Wells' early fiction. In story after story, Wells is dramatizing aspects of this conflict within himself, using his criticism of progress as a central metaphor.

The conscious awareness of this internal tension so evident in the early fiction must have come at least partly from Huxley, the militant champion of Darwin and Wells' most admired teacher. In "Evolution and Ethics" (1893), Huxley writes:

> For his successful progress, throughout the savage state, man has been largely indebted to those qualities which he shares with the ape and the tiger; his exceptional physical organization; his cunning, his sociability, his curiosity, and his imitativeness; his ruthless and ferocious destructiveness when his anger is aroused by opposition.[3]

Among civilized men, however, these animal traits are no longer useful.

> In fact, civilized man brands all these ape and tiger promptings with the name of sins; he punishes many of the acts which flow from them as crimes; and, in extreme cases, he does his best to put an end to the survival of the fittest of former days by axe and rope.[4]

Within modern man, that is to say, one current of cosmic force has set against another. The ancient law of change that shaped the human animal is now set against the newer rule that is evolving human society. In Huxley's words,

> The ethical progress of society depends, not on imitating the cosmic process, still less in running away from it, but in combating it. . . . The history of civilization details the steps by which men have succeeded in building up an artificial world within the cosmos.[5]

This unceasing conflict between the institutions of society and the original animal nature of man gave Wells a dramatic form for such novels as *The Island of Dr. Moreau* and *The Invisible Man.*

Further research in anthropology, psychology, and primate sociology has confirmed Huxley's observations. A glance at recent work in these fields will not only clarify his outline of the essential enmity between animal man and social man; it will perhaps reveal more fully the source of the tensions that have propelled modern man along the path of progress. These familiar tensions, struggling for reconciliation in the mind of the early Wells, seem to have shaped much of the early fiction, as if he had simply allowed the opposing forces in himself to seek their own form in dramatic action. Marshall D. Sahlins, a contemporary anthropologist, writes:

> The way people act, and probably have always acted, is not the expression of inherent human nature. There is a quantum difference, at points a complete opposition, between even the most rudimentary human society and the most advanced subhuman primate one.[6]

Echoing a theme from *The Island of Dr. Moreau*, he comments that human social life is determined not biologically, but culturally. This means that in the evolution of society, culture

> was forced to oppose man's primate nature on many fronts and to subdue it. It is an extraordinary fact that primate urges often become not the sure foundation of human social life, but a source of weakness in it.[7]

A somewhat more confident exponent of evolutionary progress than were the late Huxley and the early Wells, Sahlins concludes:

> In selective adaptation to the perils of the Stone Age, human society overcame or subordinated such primate propensities as selfishness, indiscriminate sexuality, dominance and brute competition. It substituted kinship and cooperation for conflict, placed solidarity over sex, morality over might. In its earliest days it accomplished the greatest reform in history, the overthrow of human primate nature, and thereby secured the evolutionary history of the species.[8]

Yet this immense leap of progress, from primate to man, was not achieved without a heavy cost, which modern man still is paying. The nature of this peculiarly human burden was made clear enough by Huxley in such essays as "Evolution and Ethics" and "The Struggle for Existence in Human Society,"[9] and by Wells in the stories to be examined below, but it has been more completely illuminated by recent research summarized by John E.

Pfeiffer.[10] The human race began, so far as we can now recon-
struct that first great act of progress, with a series of adaptations
to a drastically changed environment. The change was from forest
to grassland—a change forced perhaps by drouth that withered the
forest, perhaps by crowding from other forest dwellers. The successful adaptations included speech, erect posture, more elaborate social organization, use of tools and fire. Current studies of
two living primates, the chimpanzee and the baboon, throw new
light on these adaptations.

The chimpanzees that Jane Goodall has studied along the
northeast edge of Lake Tanganyika are believed to live much as
did our own prehuman, forest-dwelling forebears. The baboons,
though "they rank lower on the evolutionary scale and are not as
clever,"[11] are adapted to a more social life on the savannas. The
contrast between the two, revealed by field studies of the living
animals in the wild, shows something of the nature and the cost
of that act of progress that made mankind.

The chimpanzees, as Pfeiffer reports the findings of Miss
Goodall, lead a relaxed existence that "sometimes borders on
anarchy."[12] In the forest there

> are no fixed castes, no established leaders and followers. . . .
> Chimpanzees have few habits and schedules. . . . They are indi-
> vidualists supreme as, perhaps, were our ancestors.

Among the baboons on the grasslands, however, life is highly
organized. A troop of baboons is

> a close-knit, tightly ordered little cluster of monkeys. . . . Most
> troops have rigid hierarchies. . . . Clearly, in the life of the
> baboon, the community is all-important. There is no family group,
> no separate unit of father and mother and children.

The baboons "evolved in a dangerous environment where adhering
strictly to the rules was a matter of life and death. Habit is
security; novelty is suspect."[13]

Sex, more important to the baboon than to the chimpanzee, may
well have been the cohesive force that brought the free-living
forest folk together into the first human hordes—although, as
Sahlins observes, it had to be restrained as the family rose. This
view of sex as a social binding force, antagonistic to the ends
and values of the individual, is the basic theme of a whole group
of Wells' later novels, ranging from *The New Machiavelli* (1911)
to *The Research Magnificent* (1915). In these books, "men and
women are shown struggling against the dark frustrations of sex,
to realise a purpose, a form of belief, a plan of work."[14]

Though sex is not an important theme in the early fiction, except for a few satiric glances at marriage in such stories as "The Crystal Egg" and "The Purple Pileus," Wells was caught from the beginning in that universal strife between the individual and the group. From the time of his first rebellions against his mother's harsh religion and her schemes to make a draper of him, he stubbornly resented the repressive institutions of society. The idea of progress became an alluring symbol of economic and personal and sexual freedom, but his romantic individualism was always in conflict with his coolly scientific awareness of man and the cosmos. The early fiction was the mechanism with which he tried to objectify and solve this inner conflict, but the struggle lasted all his life.

In the later and weaker romance, *In the Days of the Comet*[15] first published in 1906, we find him tracing this same human burden from the prehuman past. He tells in the autobiography[16] how Land and Atkinson's *Human Origins* had showed him the role of primitive taboos in controlling male jealousy to make the first tribal societies possible. Still later, in *The Fate of Man*, he writes of

> the ever recalcitrant egotism which lies in wait for every phase of perplexity, . . . so that even leadership turns insensibly into a clamor for precedence, a jealous tyranny and the betrayal of all it set out to serve.[17]

Later yet, such hopeless cries as *The Mind at the End of Its Tether* (1945) show that this despairing awareness of the internal limits of mankind never left him. The fate of the over-shadowed individual had somehow become the fate of the race, with the idea of progress offering the last dying spark of hope against the dark tyranny of the crowd. He spent most of his later life fanning that spark, desperately but seldom very hopefully.

Huxley, by the time he became Wells' teacher, seems to have regarded the outcome of this ancient conflict with a growing doubt. As William Irvine comments in his history of the impact of evolution upon the Victorian world, "One suspects in Huxley—despite his dedicated optimism and his demonstration of clockwork harmony—a deep sense that the universe is hostile."[18] The motive behind Huxley's strenuous campaign to advance progress through better education seems to have been no serene confidence in human goodness, but rather a grim concern with human defects that must be overcome. He writes in "Agnosticism" (1889),[19] that he knows

> no study which is so unutterably saddening as that of the evolu-
> tion of humanity. . . . Out of the darkness of prehistoric ages man
> emerges with the marks of his lowly origin strong upon him. He
> is a brute, only more intelligent than the other brutes, a blind
> prey to impulses, which as often as not lead him to destruction;
> a victim to endless illusions, which make his mental existence
> a terror and a burden, and fill his physical life with barren toil
> and battle.[20]

No friend of progress-minded individuals, man

> makes a point of killing and otherwise persecuting all those who
> first try to get him to move on; and when he has moved a step,
> foolishly confers post-mortem deification on his victims. . . . The
> best men of the best epochs are simply those who make the fewest
> blunders and commit the fewest sins.[21]

Certainly Huxley himself has no illusions about the possibility
of rapid or easy progress. In "Evolution and Ethics," he somewhat gloomily observes:

> The cosmic nature born with us, and, to a large extent, necessary
> for our maintenance, is the outcome of millions of years of severe
> training, and it would be folly to imagine that a few centuries will
> suffice to subdue its masterfulness to purely ethical ends.[22]

Influenced no doubt by Huxley, both in the lecture room and
more indirectly, the early Wells seems to have felt that these
internal barriers were no more likely to yield to progress than the
external limits he had explored in *The Time Machine* and "The
Star." In "Cosmic Pessimism in H. G. Wells's Scientific Romances," Mark R. Hillegas says that these romances were intended
"to jolt the English-speaking world" out of its complacent "belief that the world would get better and better," and that Wells'
effort "took the form of imaginative presentation of Huxley's
pessimism."[23] Though this may be, it is less than all the truth.
Wells' real purpose must have been more complex, arising from a
set of contradictory attitudes that we have been exploring. Though
he may have been influenced by Huxley's pessimism, the restless
nonconformist in his being was fascinated by the forlorn hope of
progress. The problem of progress, identified with the deepset
conflicts of his own inner life, seems to have become a sort of
obsession from which he tried to free himself by allowing the
antagonistic forces to work themselves into the objective form of
the early fiction.

2   The Island of Dr. Moreau

In Wells' own words, *The Island of Dr. Moreau*[24] is "rather painful.''[25] It may be placed, along with the satires of Juvenal and Swift's account of Gulliver among the Houyhnhms, in that class of ambivalent literature in which a passionate love for a human ideal is almost obscured by an equally passionate hatred of human actuality. Although Wells lacks the complex irony of Swift, his novel has its own dark intensity. Few books have stated the native imperfections of mankind with such savage effect.

The second of the scientific fantasies, it follows *The Time Machine*. The book is based, Wells says, on an idea that he had used in an article in the *Saturday Review*.[26] Dr. Moreau, a vivisectionist, employs surgery, chemistry, and hypnotism to transform animals into semihuman beings. In a preface, Wells describes the novel as ''an exercise in youthful blasphemy,'' adding that

> now and then, though I rarely admit it, the universe projects itself towards me in a hideous grimace. It grimaced that time, and I did my best to express my vision of the aimless torture in creation.[27]

The novel dramatizes Huxley's metaphor of the garden in the ''Prolegomena.'' (Published in 1894 this essay was written as an introduction to ''Evolution and Ethics,'' originally delivered as the Romanes Lecture at Oxford in 1893.) This elaborate analogy, showing how the gardener interferes with the usual processes of evolution, illustrates ''the apparent paradox that ethical nature, while born of cosmic necessity, is necessarily at enmity with its parent.''[28] The gardener suspends ''the state of nature'' in favor of ''the state of art'': he substitutes artificial selection for natural selection; he aids his selected plants in their struggle for survival. In the novel Moreau is such a gardener, interfering with natural processes to create an artificial state. When his interference ceases, the state of nature prevails again. Not only does this metaphor outline the general scheme of the novel, but various passages in the essay offer more explicit suggestions which may easily have helped to excite the imagination of Wells.

Huxley himself extends the metaphor to compare the artificial conditions of his own English garden with those which ''a shipload of English colonists'' must set up if they are to survive ''in such a country as Tasmania was,'' and goes on to suggest that unless the whole colony remains an efficient composite unit in the new struggle for survival, perhaps ''the old state of nature will have the best of it.''[29] The position of Moreau over the island is prefigured in another passage:

> Let us now imagine that some administrative authority, as far

superior in power and intelligence to men, as men are to their cattle, is set over the colony, charged . . . to assure the victory of the settlement over the antagonistic influences of the state of nature in which it is set down.[30]

Even though this supernatural administrator "might look to the establishment of . . . a true garden of Eden . . . the Eden would have its serpent" in the inevitable return of the struggle for existence.[31] The theme of the novel may have been suggested by Huxley's idea that

since law and morals are restraints upon the struggle for existence between men in society, the ethical process is in opposition to the principle of the cosmic process, and tends to the suppression of the qualities best fitted for success in that struggle.[32]

The imagery of pain which so darkens the novel may have come from the original essay, "Evolution and Ethics," where Huxley writes:

But there is another aspect of the cosmic process, so perfect as a mechanism, so beautiful as a work of art. Where the cosmopoietic energy works through sentient beings, there arises, among its other manifestations, that which we call pain or suffering. This baleful product of evolution increases in quantity and in intensity, with advancing grades of animal organization, until it attains its highest level in man.[33]

The beastliness of mankind is the theme of the novel, driven home from the very beginning. Written with an air of documentary factuality that echoes Defoe as well as Swift, the story opens with a shipwreck in the Pacific. The narrator, a former biology student of Huxley's named Edward Prendick, survives after the wreck in a dinghy with two other men. By the eighth day of drifting, almost without water, his companions have been reduced by thirst to attempted murder and cannibalism. So superficial is civilization.

Prendick is picked up by the aptly named *Ipecacuanha*, the schooner upon which Moreau's assistant, Montgomery, is ferrying a new shipment of experimental animals to the island laboratory. The schooner's captain, a man somewhat less human than the creations of Moreau, sets Prendick adrift again near the island, leaving him Moreau's unwelcome guest.

Wells creates an atmosphere of dark horror and desperate adventure with the smoking jungle of this volcanic island, with Prendick's glimpses of the shambling, enigmatic Beast Folk, with the ominous behavior of Montgomery and Moreau, with the unendurable screaming of a puma under vivisection. Misunderstanding what he sees and hears, Prendick suspects at first that Moreau is vivisecting men. He attempts to escape, hides among the half-human creations of the knife, and is finally recaptured by Moreau, who explains his work. After Moreau's death, his creatures slowly revert toward their original bestial forms, losing their human habits and characteristics. In an ending that recalls Gulliver's discovery, on his return, that all human beings are Yahoos, Prendick, back among civilized men, is haunted by the conviction that they are another Beast People, "animals half-wrought into the outward image of human souls" (Ch. 22). He is obsessed with a dread that the people around him will begin to revert.

These Beast People have nearly all the human flaws of Swift's Yahoos. They are filthy, stupid, furtively cunning. In the final reversion, they exhibit revolting traits of the animals from which they had been made. The Monkey Man chatters resoundingly empty "big thinks" (Ch. 22), and the Leopard Man, dehumanized by the taste of blood, stalks Prendick through the jungle. There are reverting Wolf Women, Bull Men, and the odious Hyaena-Swine, all presented with a shrewd verisimilitude and a vast narrative gusto.

> So, panting, tumbling against rocks, torn by brambles, impeded by ferns and weeds, I helped to pursue the Leopard Man who had broken the Law, and the Hyaena-Swine ran, laughing savagely, by my side (Ch. 16).

The one striking difference between the Yahoos and the Beast Folk is in sexuality. Swift makes sex, next to filth, the most disgusting trait of the Yahoos. Wells merely mentions sex. The Beast People under Moreau do marry and bear offspring: creatures which he uses as material for more vivisection. Reverting, they abandon marriage; and some of them, the females first, begin "to disregard the injunction of decency" (Ch. 21). There is nothing more explicit. The reason for Wells' restraint may lie in his own tolerant attitudes toward sex, or perhaps in a prudent desire not to shock his Victorian readers—even as it stands, the novel horrified many reviewers.[34]

From the first chapter, when Prendick and his two shipwrecked companions hand halfpence to determine which shall die to feed the others, Wells emphasizes the government of the cosmos by chance.[35] Chance brings Prendick to the island. Chance has ruined Montgomery. Chance dictates most of the plot action, as when an upset lamp burns the laboratory. This reign of chance, of course, is itself an external limit upon the hope of human progress, but it also sets internal limits. Moreau, asked why he models his creations upon the human form, confesses that he chose it by chance (Ch. 14). Men, that is to say, are not made in the image of God; the human pattern, through the mechanisms of heredity and evolution, is thrown together by chance. Human strength and human weakness, human goodness and human evil, human survival and human death, are all alike the outcome of chance. Prendick escapes from the island, at the end of the book, through another unlikely freak of chance; his old enemy, the captain of the *Ipecacuanha*, arrives dead in a drifting boat in which Prendick puts back to sea.

Dr. Moreau is a rather complex symbol, at one level almost coequal with chance. Most obviously, as creator of the Beast Folk and ruler of the microcosmic island, he is God. In the autobiography, Wells tells how his religious faith was shattered when he was eleven or twelve years old by a nightmare in which "there was Our Father in a particularly malignant phase, busy roasting a poor broken sinner rotating slowly over a fire built under the wheel." He says that he saw no Devil in the dream. "My mind in its simplicity went straight to the responsible fountain head. . . . Never had I hated God so intensely."[36] When he speaks of *The Island of Dr. Moreau* as "an exercise in youthful blasphemy,"[37] he is doubtless thinking of this divine aspect of his protagonist. On the one hand, Moreau is the gravely courteous gentleman, concerned about the comfort and the safety of his uninvited guest, willing even to explain his work. But, with the same self-contradiction that had baffled the young Wells, he is the merciless vivisector, "the One with the Whip," whose ill-formed creatures worship him with a satiric litany:

"*His* is the House of Pain.

"*His* is the Hand that makes.

"*His* is the Hand that wounds.

"*His* is the Hand that heals. . . .

"*His* are the stars in the sky" (Ch. 12).

But this sardonic expression of Wells' old resentment at what he felt was divine hypocrisy is only a part of Dr. Moreau. At another level, Moreau is an ambiguous portrait of the scientist as planner of progress. Fragments of his appearance, personality, and history seem to have been taken from Huxley, whom Wells had

known as another aging and somewhat imperious biologist. Both
Huxley and Moreau have the same sense of power, the same right-
eous devotion to truth, the same stern inclination toward destruction. After an interview with Huxley in 1886, Beatrice Potter,
later Mrs. Sidney Webb, wrote of him in her diary:

> As a young man, though he felt no definite purpose in life he felt
> power. . . . He is a leader of men. . . . He is truthloving, his love
> of truth finding more satisfaction in demolition than in construc-
> tion.[38]

As Wells knew Huxley,

> he was a yellow-faced, square-faced old man, with bright little
> brown eyes, lurking as it were in caves under his heavy grey
> eyebrows, and a mane of grey hair brushed back from his wall
> of forehead, [who] lectured in a clear firm voice without hurry
> and without delay.[39]

Moreau, a white-haired man "with a fine forehead and rather heavy
features" (Ch. 6), has the same sort of self-confidence, the same
firm and steady voice. Like Huxley again, Moreau has been attacked by anti-vivisectionists (Ch. 7).

But the differences between the portrait and the model are
even more significant. More humane than Moreau, Huxley had been
able to convince Lord Shaftesbury and his other critics that he
advocated no cruelty to animals. "Like Charles Darwin," his son
testifies, he was in fact fond of animals, and "he never followed
any line of research involving experiments on living and conscious animals."[40] Huxley writes in "Autobiography" that all
of his life he has been "most unfortunately sensitive to the dis-
agreeables which attend anatomical pursuits."[41] The figure of
Moreau, on the other hand, seems almost deliberately calculated
to arouse anti-vivisectionists; exposed by an enterprising journalist in a pamphlet called "The Moreau Horrors," he has been
"simply howled" out of England (Ch. 7). Huxley had been an idol
of Wells, the scientist as intellectual liberator.[42] Moreau, on the
other hand, is the scientist as Lucifer or Frankenstein, whose
final destruction is the fitting penalty for his impious meddling
into forbidden secrets. As the ambiguous image of science, Moreau forces a sort of progress upon his island, but the changes he
engineers are undesired, pointless, and temporary. Calmly ignoring the unspeakable agony of his victims, he abandons them after
they have left his laboratory. Symbolically, at the end he is killed
by the escaping Puma Woman.

At another and even more significant level of symbolism,

Moreau is neither the Hebrew God of vengeance, nor the symbol of fallible human science. He is Nature. In the microcosm, his will is natural law. His only purpose, which is totally unrelated to the feelings or the welfare of his creatures, is "to find out the extreme limit of plasticity in a living shape" (Ch. 14). He is as amoral as the cosmos. In his own words,

> To this day I have never troubled about the ethics of the matter. The study of Nature makes a man at last as remorseless as Nature. I have gone on, not heeding anything but the question I was pursuing, and the material has . . . dripped into the huts yonder.

A symbol of the cosmic force of organic evolution, Moreau shapes his creations "in the bath of burning pain," and he is utterly indifferent to their fate.

At all these levels, Moreau exists as a blackly pessimistic comment on the whole idea of progress. As God, he is wantonly cruel and uncaring. As the human manager of progress, he is trying "to burn out the animal," to create "a rational creature" of his own, but he always fails.

> They build themselves their dens, gather fruit and pull herbs—marry, even. But I can see through it all, see into their very souls, and see there nothing but the souls of beasts, beasts that perish—anger, and the lusts to live and gratify themselves (Ch. 14).

The ineradicable animal taint corrupts all his creations, and finally kills him. As Nature, he causes infinite suffering in a cosmos where blind fate, a vast and pitiless mechanism, "seems to cut and shape the fabric of existence" (Ch. 16), and where survival or death is finally determined by chance alone.

Montgomery is a more tantalizing figure than Moreau. He is the civilized man destroyed by his own animal nature. "A youngish man with flaxen hair" and "watery expressionless eyes" (Ch. 2), he had been a London medical student until he was forced into exile merely by chance, after he happened to lose his head "for ten minutes on a foggy night" (Ch. 5). A sort of Christ to Moreau's God, he fraternizes with the Beast People and attempts to teach them. As Moreau says, "He's ashamed of it, but I believe he half likes some of these beasts" (Ch. 14). Though he retains the human warmth that Moreau lacks, he is a weakling—perhaps because humaneness is weak. He drinks. After Moreau's death, he goes on a "bank holiday," sharing his brandy with M'Ling, the Bear Man that is "the only thing that had ever really cared for him" (Ch. 19). Killed at last by his brutal companions—or perhaps by his own compassion—Montgomery dies murmuring, "The last of this silly universe. What a mess—" The ugly futility of his death is illuminated by the cold splendor of inhuman nature: the rising sun falls "like a glory upon his death-shrunken face" (Ch. 19).

Wells' satire in the novel is aimed not only at the animal nature of man, but at the folly and futility of human institutions. The Monkey Man has "a fantastic trick of coining new words" and likes to gabble about names that mean nothing (Ch. 21). The law is as useless as learning against the reverting beast. "Not to go on all-Fours; *that* is the Law. Are we not Men? . . . Not to Claw Bark of Trees; *that* is the Law. Are we not Men?" (Ch. 12). Religion is no better. The divinity of Dr. Moreau does not save him from the Puma Woman. Nor does it help Prendick, when he attempts to keep the Beast People in subjection with the desperate fiction that Moreau is not dead. "Even now he watches over us. . . . The House of Pain will come again" (Ch. 21). Reduced to the scale of the island microcosm, learning and law and religion become pathetic absurdity.

As a further irony, Wells shows that the good in human nature is no more availing than the bad. The tragic flaw that splits the microcosm is, in fact, human benevolence. Montgomery dies of kindness. The Dog Man, loyal to Prendick, regresses with the others; still faithful, he is killed by the Hyaena-Swine. But it is Prendick himself, the enlightened humanitarian, who brings about the catastrophe. As Anthony West writes,

> The disaster. . . is the consequence of turning loose the liberated intellect. . . . It overthrows the crudely effective theocracy and releases the animals from their bondage of pain and terror in the hope that it is setting them free for the pursuit of happiness.

They use their freedom, however, only to revert to savagery. "The enlightened intruder can only appeal to their better natures—a useless course as they do not have any such." [43] Thus Prendick, the image of rational science and human benevolence, appears as the final ironic symbol of self-defeating progress. Acting with the best of intentions to aid the creatures of the island, he causes first their horrible regression and then their destruction.

All these internal weaknesses of men, seen from the mechanistic viewpoint, are simply reflections of an external cosmos which has no bias in favor of goodness. The final failure of Prendick's effort at advancement, no less than the rage of the half-made Puma Woman or the blood-lust of the Leopard Man or Montgomery's chance blunder in the fog, is simply another consequence of this blindly indifferent cosmos. West comments that

Wells' pessimistic theme is "a kind of treason" to Huxley, who had tried to build a new intellectual foundation for the old moral values. As West states this theme,

> The consequence of the Darwinian intellectual revolution—with its establishment of the mechanistic view of the universe on a solid basis of observed fact—will be a moral collapse.[44]

Wells dramatizes the causes for this collapse with a grim conviction, discovering them in benevolence rather than in more obvious human faults, in the institutions of society as well as in the brute nature of humanity.

The dramatic tension of the book arises largely from the conflict between enlightened reason and primitive emotion. The idea of progress appears here, as elsewhere, to have become a part of this basic conflict, in ways of which Wells himself perhaps was not entirely conscious. Moreau is pure reason, striving with his "bath of burning pain" to consume all the "cravings, instincts, desires" that make his victims creatures of feeling. Progress is presented as an ill-fated effort to advance civilization by eliminating the animal nature of mankind. Scientific reason is the agent of progress; primitive emotion is the enemy of society, which reason must subdue. Original sin must be overcome by the enlightened will: that was the essence of the traditional religion, which Wells had consciously rejected but not completely escaped. Writing this story must have been a means of giving such old conflicts a comfortable distance. To Wells the biologist, reason is no better than feeling; his intellectual Martians are no nobler than their terrestial victims, and his Puma Woman has the same right to survive as does Dr. Moreau.

Even the island setting is ironical, West suggests, because so many eighteenth-century romances about the natural goodness of man had been set on tropical islands. Against this conventional romantic backdrop, Wells

> bleakly puts forward the classical view of man as a creature only able to rise above his brutish defects under some system of restraints and goads.[45]

In this grim world, charity is a flaw as fatal as stupidity or treachery or cruelty. It is the arrival of Prendick, the modern man of rational good will, that shatters Moreau's symbolic microcosm. Prendick himself reverts at the end, the progressive scientist slipping back toward the ancestral brute. "I am told that even now my eyes have a strange brightness, a swift alertness of movement" (Ch. 21).

3 The Invisible Man

The Invisible Man is a parable of man's inner conflict: of animal man against social man. Griffin (even his name is symbolic of his nonhuman nature) is the utter individualist, the primitive animal. In the words of Kent, the contrasting social man, "He's mad, inhuman. He is pure selfishness. He thinks of nothing but his own advantage, his own safety" (Ch. 25). He has sought invisibility as a cloak of immunity against all the sanctions of society. In pursuit of purely selfish goals, "he has cut himself off from his kind." He has betrayed and destroyed his father (Ch. 19). He has left behind a girl he had known. He lives in complete isolation, and dies at war with his species. The strichnine that he takes as a tonic is a striking symbol of his nature. "It's the devil," Kemp informs him. "It's the palaeolithic in a bottle" (Ch. 20).

Wells' special concern in *The Invisible Man*, as in "The Country of the Blind,"[46] is with the role of the intellect. No romantic, Wells does not expect human reason to be a source of truth and goodness.[47] Griffin is presented as the symbol of pure— and purely selfish—intelligence. His fine brain is simply a useful weapon in the struggle for survival, as amoral as the larger brains of Wells' Martians in *The War of the Worlds* and the even huger brain of the Grand Lunar in *First Men in the Moon*.[48] Intelligence, like any other adaptation, has biological utility only so long as it enables its owner to compete more efficiently. In the case of the Martians, even an enormous brain is not immune to decay. In the case of man, such a mind as Griffin's is equally vulnerable, because group survival requires that individual intelligence, no less than emotion, must yield to the institutions of society. A solitary human intellect is no more viable than a solitary hand or gland or cell. Anthony West comments that Griffin's invisibility, like the sight of Nuñez in "The Country of the Blind," is "symbolic of intellectual isolation," and adds that "in both stories men are absolutely corrupted in the sense that they have special knowledge that others do not share."[49]

The Invisible Man, like *The War of the Worlds*, was planned and written at Woking, where Wells had moved with his second wife early in 1895.[50] Published as a book in September, 1897,[51] it shows more careful writing than most of Wells' later work; he told an interviewer that the finished version of 55,000 words had been cut down from an earlier draft of about 100,000.[52] Although some readers have been critical, it is actually among the best of

Wells' scientific fantasies in terms of literary craftsmanship. The plot has the simplicity of classic tragedy: Griffin uses his amazing invention to make war upon the human race, and he is destroyed by the inevitable consequences of that action. The stark economy of the plot is marred by no conventional melodrama or sentimentality. Griffin's incredible feats are made acceptable by ingenious explanations and a skillful presentation. The strange is deftly interwoven with the known. The contrast of everyday places and people against Griffin's symbolic inhumanity is particularly effective; the Sussex background is solidly believable, and such comic figures as Mr. Thomas Marvel seem worthy of Dickens.

If readers tend to find fault,[53] the reason may lie partly in this very artistic perfection. Wells sticks uncompromisingly to his theme that the isolated human animal must yield to society or die. The trouble may be that, even after half a million years of necessary repetition, this sound moral lesson is still painful to each new individual. As primitive egoists, we want to sympathize with Griffin. We can't help taking some guilty share in his wild schemes for a selfish victory over the collective will. Relentlessly, however, Wells shows that his untamed self-regard, like our own, is doomed. Logically and morally, we are convinced. Yet secretly, like the comic tramp who tries to steal Griffin's invention for himself, we long for the power of invisibility: for personal independence from the old oppression of the crowd.

Most of the critical quibbles stem from the way Wells handles the point of view. The simple events of Griffin's tragic fall are presented indirectly. Except for a few chapters (19-23) in which he is telling Kemp how he made his remarkable discovery and launched his private war against mankind, we see the action through the eyes of society, from the collective viewpoint of various minor characters. With this social point of view, the effect of the novel is deliberately comic, rather than tragic, until near the end. Wells seizes eagerly upon these comic possibilities to draw a whole series of richly human figures—all selfishly antisocial enough to be convincing, but all inevitably united in the act of social revenge against the supreme selfishness of Griffin. Although this management of the narrative seems "clumsy" to Bergonzi, it would be hard to improve. Wells has at least two good reasons for avoiding Griffin's point of view. First, the use of Griffin's viewpoint would have cost him all of the mystery, surprise, and suspense of the earlier part of the story, in addition to most of the satiric comedy. Equally important, it would have cost him the best symbolism of Griffin's isolation—for Griffin's remoteness from the reader is symbolic of his denial of society.

Griffin, with his native animal egoism, could hardly have observed all the vividly detailed and richly peopled Sussex background that redeems the fairy-tale notion of invisibility.

> It was the finest of all possible Whit-Mondays, and down the village street stood a row of nearly a dozen booths and a shooting gallery, and on the grass by the forge were three yellow and chocolate waggons and some picturesque strangers of both sexes putting up a cocoanut shy. The gentlemen wore blue jerseys, the ladies white aprons and quite fashionable hats with heavy plumes. Wodger of the Purple Fawn and Mr. Jaggers the cobbler, who also sold second-hand ordinary bicycles, were stretching a string of union-jacks and royal ensigns (which had originally celebrated the Jubilee) across the road (Ch. 7).

Griffin as observer could not have seen such a background with this objective detachment, or with this robust affection.

The common reader may object that the story has no really sympathetic characters. Griffin is the enemy of all, but his opponents are no more likeable. The minor characters, the grasping landlady and the curious clockmaker, the ignorant vicar and the bumbling general practitioner, are all satirized types, unsympathetic almost by definition. Thomas Marvel, at the end, is poring over Griffin's stolen papers and dreaming Griffin's selfish dream. Kemp, the scientist as social man, shows a mean duplicity in his attempt to betray Griffin to the police. But each act of animal selfishness or of social vengeance offers its own support to the theme. The inclusion of an unselfish hero or a lovable heroine would have violated Wells' basic statement about the brutal nature of mankind.

More obviously than most of the other "scientific romances," the novel is a fantasy. As Wells himself comments, he is dealing in these stories not like Jules Verne with the actual possibilities of progress, but rather with the type of fantasy that humanizes an arbitrary fantastic notion by "translation into commonplace terms and a rigid exclusion of other marvels from the story."[54] Though his scientific patter is cleverly designed to make Griffin's tragedy plausible, he clearly feels no need to be really logical. Merely for the sake of the plot, he glosses over two serious logical inconsistencies: Griffin's lack of invisible clothing, and Griffin's ability to see.

Griffin's first test of his new secret makes a bit of white wool invisible (Ch. 20). He could clearly have provided himself with clothing made of such stuff, but inexplicably he does not. Instead he goes naked through the story, exposed to the weather, suffering from colds, risking his secret to find shelter. All this provides a powerful symbolic support for the theme. It makes him the animal man, "just a human being—solid, needing food and drink, needing covering, too." Lacking the invisible garments and equipment he might have provided himself, he is "wandering, mad with rage, naked, impotent" (Ch. 9). This predicament, which determines the whole action of the plot and finally brings about the tragic fall of the Invisible Man, is dramatically effective but logically unsupported. As pure intellect, Griffin might have planned his war against the species with more intelligence.

With the same dramatic license, Wells ignores the fact that an invisible man would be blind. As he admitted to Arnold Bennett,

Any alteration of the refractive index of the eye lenses would make vision impossible. Without such alteration the eyes would be visible as glassy globules. And for vision it is also necessary that there should be visual purple behind the retina and an opaque cornea and iris. On these lines you would get a very effective short story but nothing more.[55]

But the plot requires Griffin to see, as well as to go naked. Coolly forgetting inconsistencies, Wells achieves his aim: "the same amount of conviction as one gets in a good gripping dream."[56]

A complex metaphor, Griffin reveals the lawless primitive ego still surviving in the most advanced of men. Though he is the symbol of science, his mastery of nature is always a tool of selfish personal power, never an aid to the race. At the beginning he keeps his research secret because he will not share the credit with his professor (Ch. 19); at the end he is trying to inaugurate a private Reign of Terror against mankind (Ch. 23). His invisibility, like his superior brain, is simply another device for private survival, as inherently selfish as a longer fang or a sharper claw. Symbolically, at the instant of his discovery, he is alone. "The laboratory was still, with the tall lights burning brightly and silently. In all my great moments I have been alone" (Ch. 19). The discovery brings him a vision of pure ego set free from society. "A shabby, poverty-struck, hemmed-in demonstrator, teaching fools in a provincial college," he sees "all that invisibility might mean to a man—the mystery, the power, the freedom."

Though Griffin is at first aware of no limits to his new power, his fate is soon foreshadowed in a revealing dream. Sleeping in an emporium where he has found one night's refuge, he dreams that he is back at his father's funeral, being forced into the open grave. He shouts for help, but the droning clergyman and the mourners ignore him.

> I realized that I was invisible and inaudible. . . . I struggled in vain, I was forced over the brink, the coffin rang hollow as I fell upon it, and the gravel came flying after me in spadefuls. Nobody heeded me, nobody was aware of me. I made convulsive struggles and awoke (Ch. 22).

Ignoring this clear warning that the penalty for isolation will be death, Griffin wages his solitary war to the end. In a memorably vivid passage, his dying body becomes visible. "First came the little white nerves, a hazy grey sketch of a limb, then the glassy bones and intricate arteries, then the flesh and skin" (Ch. 28). Dead, the animal man returns to society: "the bruised and broken body of a young man about thirty . . . his eyes wide open, and his expression . . . one of anger and dismay." Covered with a sheet, he is carried into the Jolly Cricketers.

As the instrument of progress, Griffin illustrates the paradox that the impulse toward advancement springs from a regressive animal individualism rather than from the social nature that makes us human. Social institutions are, in fact, necessarily conservative; only the individual intellect can initiate progressive change. Wells is reminding us, however, that changes initiated by such anti-social instruments as Griffin do not inevitably tend toward the ultimate human good. As Wells' image of the scientist, Griffin belongs with Nebogipfel and Dr. Moreau. He is the scientist not as the benign engineer of progress, but as demon and destroyer. In him, Bergonzi suggests, "Wells seems to have brought the type to final realization before imaginatively casting him out of his consciousness." [57]

Thus the book records another step in Wells' mental evolution. Griffin is more than a literary character; he is an expression of the romantic egoist in Wells himself. Bergonzi interprets him as a scapegoat figure hunted out of society, adding that

> it is perhaps not altogether fanciful to suppose that what is being "cast out" is not merely the dangerous pretensions of contemporary science, but also the young Wells's own identification with a highly romanticized kind of scientist-magician.[58]

Griffin's tragic fall seems to reflect Wells' reluctant acceptance of the classic view that the evil nature of the individual requires social restraint. The dramatizations of Wells' own internal conflicts in these early stories may have been a kind of catharsis that left him free to undertake all his later campaigns to further the advancement of mankind.

Commenting on these changes in Wells' outlook, Bergonzi writes:

> By the early years of this century [his] utopian and positivist convictions were coming increasingly to dominate his earlier intellectual skepticism and his imaginative attachment to the traditional patterns of southern English life.[59]

He observes that Wells was certainly aware of his conflict when, in the twenties, he wrote of himself: "Temperamentally he is egoistic and romantic, intellectually he is clearly aware that the egoistic and the romantic must go."[60] Doubtless the writing of such books as *The Island of Dr. Moreau* and *The Invisible Man* helped Wells to reach this self-awareness. Certainly both novels owe their form and effect largely to the freedom which he allowed his own discordant attitudes to express themselves in objective dramatic action: Griffin seems at least as vital an element of Wells as does Kemp, the social man whose mind can travel "into a remote speculation of social conditions of the future" and lose "itself at last over the time dimension" (Ch. 17). In any case, both novels are clearly related to the problem of progress. In *The Invisible Man*, just as emphatically as in *The War of the Worlds* although from a different point of view, Wells is pointing out the evolutionary legacies that inevitably turn utopian hopes into cruel illusions.

4   "The Country of the Blind" and Other Stories

Wells seems more deeply concerned with the internal than the external limits to progress, perhaps for two reasons. As the literary artist, he finds the internal struggle more complex, more appealing than the conflict with the external cosmos. As the prophet of progress, he is more hopeful of doing something about the human limits. The probable life of the solar system cannot be extended by any predictable human exertion; and no competing species, Martian or terrestial, now seems more dangerous to future human progress than does man himself. But the human limits seem to merit more attention. Not only are they nearer, but they seem to offer tantalizing possibilities of being somehow widened or removed by human knowledge and intelligence.

The short stories, though of course not deliberately planned to develop any common theme, do reflect Wells' early preoccupation with these human limits. Most of them were written before his rebellion against literary form; they are amazingly inventive, fully imagined, lively in style. A bright kaleidoscope of comic and tragic and tragicomic moods, they offer such richly varied glimpses and interpretations of life that classification is difficult and generalization dangerous. Still the literary artist, not yet the high priest of social reform through rational enlightenment, Wells is a perceptive critic of mankind. The elemental conflict between animal man and social man appears again and again, not because he has any thematic axe to grind, but simply because this conflict is the inevitable root of character and drama, because it creates the basic irony of life.

Like the novels, the short stories show a maturing ability to see this conflict as comedy. In Wells' own evolution, the most striking change at this period is shift from the tragic to the comic mood. The process, however, is not quite that simple. A shift from emotional identification to intellectual detachment, it does not always mean a growth of optimism, for detachment lends itself to satire, which more than tragedy is the natural vehicle of pessimism. Nor was the change ever entirely definite or complete. "The Stolen Bacillus," one of the very first short stories, is a comic farce. The lightly comic *Wheels of Chance* and the darkly tragic *Island of Dr. Moreau* were written at about the same time. Comedy and tragedy are mixed in *The Invisible Man*. Some of Wells' last stories, "A Dream of Armageddon" (1903), "The Country of the Blind" (1904), and "The Door in the Wall" (1906), are tragedies. Yet, in spite of such ambiguous evidence, the change seems real enough. Wells' talent for realistic comedy, visible from the beginning, developed steadily until it found its most mature expression in *The History of Mr. Polly* (1909). Griffin, however, is the last major hero of the classic tragic type. The later tragic heroes represent a different pattern.

In the tragic figures of Griffin's type, Wells is criticizing the individual. In the comedies, as in the later tragedies, he shifts his fire to society. The conflict is the same; the viewpoint and effects are different. In the old war between the individual and society, neither side is right or wrong; that is the basic human irony. It is only some excess that makes a tragic flaw, for all men are individuals, inheriting animal traits through the genes just as inevitably as they inherit social traits through the culture. And these animal traits are vital; sacrificing too many of them is just as suicidal as sacrificing too few.

The comic hero, like the tragic, is an individual in revolt against society—a total conformist would be no hero. The difference is that the selfish tragic hero is destroyed for yielding too little to the mandates of society, while the comic hero is ultimately rewarded for resisting the collective selfishness that would make him yield too much. The tragic hero is the aggressor against the group. The comic hero is the victim. With the conflict forced upon him, he must at last revolt to save his own vital spark of self. In such stories as "The Purple Pileus" and "The Crystal Egg," [61] we glimpse the germ of the same comic hero who is more fully developed in the figures of Kipps and Mr. Polly.

The later tragic heroes, Nuñez in "The Country of the Blind" and Hedon in "A Dream of Armageddon" and Wallace in "The Door in the Wall," resemble the comic type more than they do Griffin. Although each of them displays ego enough to make him convincingly alive, they are the defenders, not the attackers, in the inevitable clash with the crowd. What each defends in his own way is an individual freedom more precious than survival through conformity. In each of them, the essential traits of individual selfishness are overshadowed by an overwhelming collective selfishness. In each case, the tragic ending results from a choice that proves the vital worth of self.

Wells' favorite fiction pattern brings everyday reality into collision with something exotic. The familiar element in this group of stories is usually provided by the institutions and pressures of society. The fantastic element is often some device which allows the hero at least a glimpse of individual freedom. In the comic versions of the pattern, the hero makes some kind of escape. In the tragic version, his excessive individualism results in his destruction.

"The Diamond Maker" [62] illustrates the tragic pattern. The hero is another Griffin: a selfish and solitary individualist who finds a way of making artificial diamonds. Because of his self-centered greed, which he sees reflected in the competitive society in which he lives, he works in secret. Successful, he finds himself a social outcast, unable to benefit from his discovery. Carrying a fortune in diamonds around his neck, he can find neither food nor shelter.

Another tragedy, "The Cone," [63] shows Wells' early recognition of this human conflict as a barrier to progress, and also his early awareness of "the conflict of the two cultures." [64] Written before the final revision of The Time Machine, it is "the last surviving relic . . . of what was to have been a vast melodrama, all at the same level of high sensation." [65] Horrocks, the progressive ironmaster, is pitted against a philandering aesthete. Overcome by a primitive lust for individual revenge, he burns the poet alive upon the cone that caps a blast furnace.

"The Moth"[66] might have been called "The Science Jungle." The scientist, the very agent of progress, is represented as a primitive predator. The satire on the ruthless egoism of scientific controversy anticipates the savage quarrels I have seen between contemporary linguists. "The Story of the Late Mr. Elvesham"[67] is an equally striking indictment of the amorality of science; the senescent scientist steals the youthful hero's body. "The Red Room,"[68] a ghost story, displays fear itself as the primal enemy of progressive rationalism. In "The Argonauts of the Air,"[69] the progressive individual is destroyed by the pressures of conservative society: the builder of the first successful flying machine is ridiculed by the world, finally killed by his invention.

The comic version of this pattern is illustrated by "The Purple Pileus,"[70] which Wells calls "perhaps the best and reallest" of his very early stories.[71] Here he uses the method of comedy to make a pessimistic view of life endurable. The harsh facts of reality are feelingly observed and accurately reported. Mr. Coombes, the comic hero, is trapped in the institution of marriage. A small shopman, he finds his private scheme of progress thwarted by a disloyal wife, "the luxuries of divorce" out of his reach. Driven from his own home, he tries to kill himself by eating the Pileus, a poisonous-looking fungus. The ensuing episode, in which the effects of this dangerous meal restore him to the mastery of his fate, is not only successful comedy but also, because of the very improbability of this kind of escape from social compulsion, an ironic restatement of his predicament. Fighting to preserve his essential self, the comic hero is made sympathetic by the shadow of the greater collective selfishness that he must defy.

"The Stolen Bacillus,"[72] the first of the "single sitting stories" that Wells "ground out" for £5 each,[73] is a cheerful burlesque upon the ironic limitations of a typical promoter of progress: an anarchist whose unchecked individualism betrays him into a fantastic attempt to infect the city water supply with cholera germs. "The Apple"[74] follows the same comic pattern; the hero is a young student who sacrifices progress upon the altar of social conformity when he throws away a magic fruit from the Tree of Knowledge because it would make an unsightly bulge in his pockets.

"The Man Who Could Work Miracles,"[75] which Wells later rewrote as a film play,[76] gives a comic twist to the theme of *The*

Island of Dr. Moreau. A skeptical young clerk, George McWhirter Fotheringay, finding that he has an unexpected miraculous gift, calls upon his pastor to help him hasten progress. They reform drunkards, change beer and alcohol to water, improve railway service, drain a swamp, enrich the soil on One Tree Hill, and cure the vicar's wart. Seeking more time for progress, they stop the earth's rotation—with cataclysmic consequences. Thus, as in *The Island of Dr. Moreau*, the benevolent effort to aid progress ends in disaster. For all its good humor, the story is darkly pessimistic. Bad as the world may be, human enlightenment can only make it worse.

"A Dream of Armageddon"[77] is a tragedy of self against society, more complex and intellectual than *The Invisible Man*. Hedon's refusal to sacrifice personal love to public duty is followed by a holocaust that he might have prevented, and by his own destruction. Yet he seems more like the comic heroes than like Griffin, because the Armageddon is not of his making. Sex in this story is an element of the essential self, not its enemy, as it becomes in the later marriage novels.[78] Hedon's selfish passion is overshadowed by the destructive collective selfishness around him, and his death for love seems a sort of victory.

Between "A Dream of Armageddon" and "The Country of the Blind,"[79] the role of love is neatly reversed. Love to Hedon is the vital expression of self, worth more than even the survival of society. Love to Nuñez is the enemy of self, the most powerful force crushing him toward conformity. "The Country of the Blind" is one of Wells' finest stories, and perhaps his most mature and sophisticated survey of the universal conflict of self against society.

The story must have grown out of Wells' simpler study of the same theme in *The Invisible Man*. In that novel, describing his early mood of selfish elation, Griffin says, "I felt as a seeing man might do, with padded feet and noiseless clothes, in a city of the blind." Later, becoming aware of the tragic consequences of his intellectual solitude, he says, "I saw . . . a blind man approach me, and fled limping, for I feared his subtle intuitions" (Ch. 21). Nuñez, the seeing man among the blind, is at the beginning somewhat like Griffin, planning to use his unique advantage selfishly, but the development of the story shows a significant change in Wells' attitudes toward both sex and self.

Nuñez is the romantic individualist, his sight the symbol of self and the agent of progress. He falls into an isolated Andean valley where a blind tribe has been isolated for fifteen generations.

With a flash of Griffin's tragic ambition, he recalls an old proverb, "In the Country of the Blind the One-eyed Man is King."[80] The blind folk, however, shatter all his selfish dreams. They are society. Their world is small, static, closed, comfortably urban. They adhere to a classic theory of the innate evil of man. "Our fathers have told us men may be made by the forces of Nature," Nuñez is informed. "It is the warmth of things and moisture, and rottenness—rottenness."[81] Refusing to believe what he says he can see, they tell him that there are no mountains, that their universe, at first an empty hollow in the rocks, is now covered with a smooth stone roof from which the dew and the avalanches fall. Two original minds in the past, sent as Wells says by "the chance of birth and heredity"[82] had been agents of progress among them, but now they are middle-class conservatives, their stable ways of life fixed by tradition, supported by learning, sanctioned by religion.

Nuñez's talk of sight is not only incomprehensible but blasphemous. His attempt to use force is a failure. He soon abandons his egoistic ambition to be king, but Wells has not yet finished this dramatic analysis of the worth of self. Reduced to slavery, Nuñez falls in love with a blind girl, Medina-saroté. The match is opposed because the blind regard him as "a being apart, an idiot, incompetent thing below the permissible level of a man."[83] A blind doctor proposes at last to cure him of the disease of sight.

"Those queer things that are called the eyes, and which exist to make an agreeable soft depression in the face, are diseased . . . in such a way as to affect his brain."[84]

For the girl's sake, Nuñez consents at first to the surgical removal of these irritant bodies. When the day comes, however, he looks upward at the beauty of the morning, with the sun above upon the slopes of ice and snow, and begins "very circumspectly" to climb.

When sunset came he was no longer climbing, but he was far and high. He had been higher, but he was still very high. His clothes were torn, his limbs were blood-stained, he was bruised in many places, but he lay there as if he were at ease, and there was a smile on his face.[85]

As the symbol of self, Nuñez's sight, like Hedon's lady, is more precious than life. Even though Nuñez should die where he lies "peacefully contented under the cold stars," his death is not defeat but victory.[86]

"The Country of the Blind" is by no means simply a tract on progress. It is a complex aesthetic creation, rich in significance, concretely imagined, more emotional than intellectual. The seeing man, not merely a symbol of self or intelligence or progress, is also an intricate human being, haughty at the beginning with his imagined superiority, quickly responsive to visual beauty, unable to strike a blind man, capable of love, yet ready to sacrifice everything for the sight that is the metaphor of self. The closed world of the blind is fully created, from the guiding curbs along their uncluttered paths to their myth of their own creation. The dramatic tension which shapes the story arises from the antagonism between two views of life, a collision too nearly universal to be contained in any neat set of labels. It is the enmity between permanence and change, the incongruity between the poet and the plowman, the chasm between reckless youth and prudent age, the contrast between the self-directed liberalism of Wells' own father and the rigidly conforming conservatism of his mother. The story is successful because it gives an objective resolution to Wells' own conflicting attitudes toward self and society—and toward sex as an agent of society. The idea of progress is involved because society is inherently regressive and the self is the only instrument of change. The closed world of the blind rejects the instrument of progress, as in fact our real world commonly does.

This same conflict appears in many more of Wells' stories: in the complex mythical and personal symbolism of "The Door in the Wall," [87] and even in the practical jokes played upon society by the uninhibited hero of "The Triumphs of a Taxidermist." [88] The stories reflect the varied experiences of Wells' own life; the unlucky student whose moral fragility is revealed in "A Slip Under the Microscope" [89] might almost have been Wells himself. Spontaneous as dreams, produced in a mood of exuberant invention to be read for light amusement, these tales seldom display explicit thematic intentions, but the criticism of progress reappears as a persistent reflection of that central human conflict. Taken as a group, they emphasize the realistic awareness of human limitations with which Wells approached the myth of progress. Comte and Marx and Spencer planned their vast systems of reform with a lofty disregard for the human atoms involved. Wells, however, always knew that the coming world, whatever its shape, must be put together by the efforts of individual men, whose private lives are more precious than society, and whose limiting stupidity and ignorance and greed are as old and stubborn as the drive to survive.

Beyond These Limits

1 The Relativity of Progress

In spite of the limits considered above, progress does occur. A third group of Wells' stories may be read as an imaginative exploration and evaluation of it. In a 1921 short story, ''The Grisly Folk,'' he takes a backward look at the very beginning of the climb, when our own ancestors were outstripping Neanderthal man. In several stories he sets modern man against the primitive, to show progress getting nowhere. In two companion novelettes, ''A Story of the Stone Age'' and ''A Story of the Days to Come,'' he contrasts the paleolithic past with the twenty-second century, somewhat to the advantage of the past. In *When the Sleeper Wakes* he studies the same near future in more disenchanting detail. Finally, in *The First Men in the Moon*, the last of the great scientific fantasies, he considers the ultimate consequences of social evolution. In the whole group of stories, he presents a vast survey of past and future change, continued through geologic ages. Under his ambiguous study, however, the word progress becomes ironic.

In these stories Wells is weighing the fruits of progress on an ambivalent scale of values. Both scientist and humanist, he is keenly sensitive to human suffering and human aspirations. He longs for the ideal evolution that would increase the balance of

95

happiness over misery. As a biologist, however, he is compelled to see the human race as only another competitor for survival, forced to define human progress simply as better adaptation. Such a view, as he knew from the beginning, is often at odds with benevolent desires. In the early Wells at least, the biologist usually prevails over the humanist.

Literary critics have been inclined to sneer at Wells as a scientist. Clement Shorter, for example, in a review of *The Invisible Man*, refers to his "smattering of science" and says that "it was Huxley and Tyndall who made him possible, although both would have loathed his conclusions."[1] It is true as he admits that he was "rather handicapped by the irregularity and unsoundness" of his general education, and that he failed at the end of his three years as a science student in London. But the failure was not due to any intellectual incompetence. At the end of his year under Huxley, though shabby and poorly fed and housed, he was "one of the three who made up the first class."[2] His later failure seems to have been partly due to his restless impatience with teachers less able than Huxley and less brilliant than Wells himself: with Guthrie, in physics, who was "dull, slow, distraught . . . with a general effect of never having fully awakened to the universe about him,"[3] and with Judd, in geology, who "had the same lack of militant curiosity as Guthrie"[4] and who tended to over-control his students and "wanted to mess about with their minds."[5] After his failure under Judd in 1887, he was able to take first place in second-class honors at the examination for his B. Sc. degree in 1890. He later taught biology, and his first published book was a *Textbook of Biology*.[6] His early essay, "The Rediscovery of the Unique,"[7] no less than the early fiction, is evidence that Wells, perhaps better than most professional scientists, had learned the scientific method and the scientific outlook. Yet, fortunately, he never forgot what Guthrie and Judd never knew: that the dead facts of science belong to the living world of men.

Wells certainly accepted the biological view of progress as adjustment to environment. He knew that environments change, sometimes imperceptibly in a hundred million years, sometimes catastrophically. Biological progress is whatever happens to help a species keep alive and perhaps to multiply. Such a definition, of course, runs counter to any absolute evaluation of progress in terms of divine purpose or even of altruistic idealism. Biological progress is always relative to the conditions for survival. The environment may demand drastic change, or it may penalize any change at all. In his "Lectures on Evolution" (1876), Huxley comments that there are admirably preserved scorpions in the Carboniferous formations of Europe and America which "are hardly distinguishable from such as now live" and suggests that if conditions remain favorable there is no reason why such scorpions should not survive "as long as this world exists."[8]

The environment sometimes alters to favor "lower" types. In a passage in "Evolution and Ethics" which may have helped to shape the concluding chapters of *The Time Machine*, Huxley speculates that, if our planet were to cool,

> the survival of the fittest might bring about, in the vegetable kingdom, a population of more and more stunted and humbler and humbler organisms, until the "fittest" that survived might be nothing but lichens, diatoms, and such microscopic organisms as those which give red snow its color.[9]

Wells uses the same general idea at the end of *The War of the Worlds*. The Martian invaders, symbolic of the ultimate peak of human evolution, are less fit to survive than the simplest organisms.

That Wells saw progress as an unceasing process of biological adaptation is clearly evident from these two novels. The Morlocks in *The Time Machine* keep and eat the degenerate Eloi, in a symbiotic relationship that enables both subhuman species to survive. The huge crab-like monsters and the bright-green lichens and the hopping black thing that the Time Traveller sees in the remote future, long after the disappearance of mankind, are new adaptations to the changing environment of the dying earth. The Martians in *The War of the Worlds*, even at the summit of evolutionary progress, still face the eternal choice of adaptation or death. The invasion of earth is a desperate attempt to meet the environmental threat of their own cooling world. For all their advancement, the effort fails. All their millions of years of intellectual progress has not freed them from the laws of biology.[10]

Considering the possibility of a kind of progress closer to the human ideal in "Evolution and Ethics" and its "Prolegomena" (1894), Huxley discusses the "ethical process" as "the gradual strengthening of the social bond" which leads to cooperation instead of ruthless competition within each social unit.[11] He states optimistically that "much may be done to change the nature of man himself."[12] But "cosmic nature is no school of virtue,"[13] and even in society men remain subject to the cosmic process, which is opposed to goodness and virtue. So far as the ethical bond is an evolutionary device which makes the social unit fitter to survive, it too depends upon environment; it is just as relative and temporary and pragmatic as any other instrument of progress. With the same ultimate pessimism that haunted the early Wells, Huxley wrote:

> The theory of evolution encourages no millenial anticipations. If, for millions of years, our globe has taken the upward road, yet, some time, the summit will be reached and the downward route will be commenced. The most daring imagination will hardly venture the suggestion that the power and the intelligence of man can ever arrest the procession of the great year.[14]

The direction of biological progress—that is, the kind of adaptation that has favored survival—has generally been toward greater specialization. In the physical evolution of such "higher" forms as mammals, specialization of the cells created new tissues and organs and functions. In the social evolution of mankind, a similar specialization has created the functional units of society. The family, the basic social unit, was not built upon sex or even upon love, in the opinion of contemporary anthropologists; it was a device for the division of labor between men and women, a social step beyond the physical specialization of sex. "The men typically hunt and make weapons; the women gather wild plants and take care of the home and the children."[15] Wells considers the ultimate results of specialization in *The First Men in the Moon.*

This kind of progress has a long record of success, all the way from the first multicellular creature to the modern industrial assembly line, but it has been expensive. The simplest living things are normally immortal, fissioning instead of dying; having no specialized senses, they can hardly experience pain. The "higher" organisms are still paying for their past progress with suffering and death, as well as with the painful suppression of the individual self.[16] Wells reveals in *The First Men in the Moon,* more clearly perhaps than anywhere else, his feelings that these costs are intolerably high.

Such was Wells' dilemma. As a romantic individualist, as an enlightened liberal, as his father's son, he knew that the vital human values reside in the individual; he knew that society is simply a means to happiness, never an end in itself. As a realist, however, as a biological scientist, he knew that "social progress" is almost inevitably an endless surrender of individual freedoms to a more and more powerful society. Though his deepest personal reactions to that dilemma are expressed in "The Country of the Blind,"[17] the problem is explored more fully in the stories considered below.

Wells' own hopes for progress, never so completely optimistic as his critics have believed, were restrained from the beginning by his realistic awareness that ''progress'' does not equal happiness. Evolution must continue. The individuals and the social units making the more useful adjustments will continue to eliminate the less successful. Beyond that pragmatic test, however, there is no absolute. Huxley confesses

> that the violator of ethical rules constantly escapes the punishment which he deserves; that the wicked flourishes like the green bay tree, while the righteous begs his bread.[18]

Wells finds a dominant theme in this cautionary idea, that intellectual and technological and social progress are irrelevant or even hostile to the utopian ideal of universal happiness.

The life of these stories grows from a paradox: that the impulse toward progress is ultimately identical with the desire for regression. All the social institutions that were the steps on the way from ape to man have now become intensely conservative. The group mind thinks no new thoughts; it initiates no change. It is the animal self, in impulsive rebellion against the fossil past, that forever seeks freedom in change.

Social evolution has continued, during the seventy years and more since Wells wrote, much as he anticipated. The forces of change have generally sprung from the individual hunger for fulfillment. The actual result has often been erosion of individualism by the ruthless collectivism that Wells described in *The First Men in the Moon*. Most obvious under the totalitarian dictatorships, this kind of change has been the rule in ''the free world'' as well. Like Wells' baby Selenite grown in his constricting bottle, men everywhere are sacrificing individual identity for social survival. Humanists echo Wells' outcry of alarm, but they are as helpless as Graham was against Ostrog's pragmatic power in *When the Sleeper Wakes*. Even Wells' own World State, if established, would probably be one more step in the extinction of the individual. This accelerating trend toward the triumph of society over the self is neatly summarized in the following paragraph by one world leader:

> Today, individualism is in error. Everywhere the need to associate becomes increasingly patent. There is not a trade which is not becoming a corporation. The parties speak only of rules and exclusions. Sport groups its federations and trains its teams. At the same time, the agglomerated and precipitated tempo of life imposes on workshops, offices, and the street a practical discipline whose rigor would have revolted our fathers. Mechanization

and the division of labor make new inroads every day against
eclecticism and fantasy. Whatever the tasks and the conditions,
the nature of things distributes work and leisure in equal portions
to all. Education is tending to be unified, housing increasingly
uniform. From Sydney to San Francisco, via Paris, clothes are cut
according to the same pattern. Even faces are coming to look
alike. Without concluding, like Mr. Maeterlinck, that mankind is
tending toward the ant heap, it is clear that it disapproves of the
independent and the freewheeling.[19]

De Gaulle's diagnosis, like Wells' imaginative speculation,
seems more relevant today than when it was first published (1932).
Progress goes on—if defined as simply the ceaseless change that
makes survival possible. The fitness of the fittest is never absolute, but always relative to the moment alone. These stories show
the romantic idealist in Wells trying somehow to controvert or
deny or escape the consequences of this biological view of progress, but inevitably forced to accept them.

2   Evaluating Past Progress

In "The Grisly Folk,"[20] published in 1921, six months after
The Outline of History, the later Wells glances approvingly back
at early human progress. The grisly folk are Neanderthal men.
The narrative, more anthropological essay than fiction, recon-
structs the epic of their extermination by the fitter race. The
grisly folk are pictured as mute and stupid cannibals, originals
of "the legends of ogres and man-eating giants that haunt the
childhood of the world."[21] The conquerors were more highly
social, taught by their women "the primary cooperation of sonship
and brotherhood." They have the gift of speech. Fighting the
grisly men like dogs fighting a bear, "they shouted to one another
what each should do, and the Neandertaler had no speech; he did
not understand. They moved too quickly for him and fought too
cunningly." The story is interesting for its glimpse of the change
in Wells himself. Twenty years after The First Men in the Moon,
he has buried his earlier misgivings about the nature and the
value of progress. He approves this crude display of human fitness for survival without visible reservations.

The earlier Wells is not so optimistic. Evaluating ethics as
well as progress against the biological standard of survival-
value, he shows that both are relative. Several stories support
Huxley's point that the liberal idealist tends to condemn in men
what the evolutionary process has proved good in apes and tigers.
He makes a comic hero of the criminal in such tales as "Mr.

Ledbetter's Vacation''[22] and ''The Hammerpond Park Burglary.''[23] Revolt against society is justified with the lightly sarcastic argument that, since men have been degraded by civilization, the burglar is ''the only true adventurer left on earth.''[24] The same attitude recurs in *The History of Mr. Polly*. ''Arson, after all, is an artificial crime.''[25]

This same relativistic theme shapes another cluster of stories, in which Wells' narrative device of tossing something improbable into the everyday world takes the form of an impact between modern man as the familiar element and something primitive as the novelty. In ''Aepyornis Island,''[26] the modern man is cast away on an Indian Ocean atoll with an egg which hatches into an enormous prehistoric bird. Butcher, the comic and scarcely admirable symbol of modernity, is able to survive the attacks of the primitive bird, but only through the primitive elements in his own nature and by the use of a primitive device. (But Wells is writing to amuse himself and his readers, not to preach themes. In one light-hearted tale, ''The Flying Man,''[27] written under the spell of Kiping, he even lets progress triumph. A young infantry lieutenant, cornered by head-hunting savages on a high mountain ledge, escapes by applying science: he makes a parachute out of a tent.)

''The Lord of the Dynamos''[28] develops the same conflict more thoughtfully, and in a tragic mood. The electrician Holroyd embodies the worst of the scientific culture. ''A heavy, red-haired brute with irregular teeth,'' he doubts God but accepts Carnot's cycle, and has ''read Shakespeare and found him weak in chemistry.''[29] He bullies his black assistant, Azumazi, who has come to London ''to worship at the shrine of civilisation.''[30] The black man comes to adore a dynamo, as his father before him had adored a meteoric stone, and finally offers Holroyd to it as a sufficient sacrifice. Among many meanings, this powerful and intricately symbolic story points out that the materialistic progress that Europe has offered the rest of the world can be a very deadly gift, both to giver and receiver.

''The Treasure in the Forest''[31] and ''Pollock and the Porroh Man''[32] are tragic melodramas in which progress is defeated by the primitive. The degenerate moderns in the first story discover too late that the murdered Chinaman has protected his buried treasure with thorns ''similar to those the Dyaks poison and use in their blowing-tubes.''[33] Pollock, another symbol of corrupt modernity, is pursued out of Africa and finally driven to suicide. by the primitive magic of the Porroh man.

By 1903, when he wrote "The Land Ironclads," [34] Wells displays more sympathy for progress. A primitive country is at war with a progressive industrial nation. The war correspondent, a figure out of Stephen Crane, believes that in civilization, for all its suffering and injustice, there lies "something that might be the hope of the world." [35] The story accurately forecasts the deadly stalemate of trench warfare, and the invention and tactics of the tank, a prediction of which Wells was always proud. [36] The tanks defeat the primitives. The correspondent, at the end of the story, is allowed to observe that the young men

> standing about their victorious land ironclad, drinking coffee and eating biscuits, had also in their eyes and carriage something not altogether degraded below the level of a man. [37]

The companion novelettes, "A Story of the Stone Age" [38] and "A Story of the Days to Come," [39] both first published in 1897, form together a fictionized survey of human progress over a span of fifty thousand years, from the invention of the axe by the first men in England to the invention of Euthanasia by their degenerate descendents at the beginning of the twenty-second century. These stories show Wells turning to the sort of thinking that produced *When the Sleeper Wakes* and *Anticipations*. They foreshadow the later Wells, more concerned with historic and prophetic speculation that with people and their problems. Yet his attitudes are still curiously contradictory; his approving visions of past and future advancement are often blurred by misgivings that seem to spring from a romantic primitivism.

In "A Story of the Stone Age," Wells looks somewhat wistfully back at the childhood of humanity. His cave man, Ugh-lomi, is a Promethean hero of progress, [40] who not only makes the first axe but rides the first horse and kills the first cave bear. Yet, even though triumphant progress is the overt theme, the narrative is ambiguously flavored with the romantic primitivism of Kipling's *Jungle Books*. In the beginning, when the little buff-colored children of men are dabbling in the edge of the river, there is "no fear, no rivalry, and no enmity between them and the hippopotami." [41] The animals are named; they think and speak. Andoo, the cave bear, greets the fatal shape of progress with the fatuous complacency of an ursine Colonel Blimp.

> "I was never so startled in my life. . . . They are the most extraordinary beasts. Attacking *me*!"
>
> "I don't like them," said the she-bear. . . .
>
> "A feebler sort of beast I *never* saw. I can't think what the

world is coming to. Scraggy, weedy legs. . . . Wonder how they keep warm in winter?''

"Very likely they don't," said the she-bear.

"I suppose it's a sort of monkey gone wrong."

"It's a change," said the she-bear.[42]

Ugh-lomi's progressive achievements merely enable him to survive; they do not yet threaten the stability of his somewhat idyllic world. He is only slightly less inarticulate and superstitious than his fellow savages. He destroys his enemies, rescues his abducted mate, kills a man-eating lion, and fights his way to mastery of the tribe. If, at last, he himself is "killed and eaten," it is only after he has been master for many moons and has had his will in peace.[43] In this story, Wells' desire to celebrate the early triumphs of progress is at odds with a nostalgia for the primitive past. If these conflicting attitudes had been successfully embodied in antagonistic characters, they might have contributed dramatic form and effect. As they are, however, they weaken the story.

The companion novelette, "A Story of the Days to Come," begins with a satiric jab at Victorian conservatism in the person of a very proper Mr. Morris, a human Andoo, who is "one of those worthy people who take no interest in the future of mankind at all."[44] A nearly identical descendent, in the twenty-second century, is the principal villain of the conventional melodrama in which Wells has clothed his study of the world to come: the same disturbing world described in *When the Sleeper Wakes* and "A Dream of Armageddon."[45]

Mwres, as the future Mr. Morris spells his name, is attempting to force his daughter to marry a worn-out playboy named Bindon. She and young Denton, her true love, are misplaced primitives who affect the archaic art of reading and seek escape from the commonplace wonders of their daily lives into historical romances of the fine old times of Queen Victoria the Good. When the villainous father hires a hypnotist to erase Denton from her mind, the young man rescues her and has her memory restored. Persecuted by the father and Bindon, the penniless young lovers are driven first out into the open country and then down through the class levels of the enormous city.

The escape into the vacant country is an excursion into primitivism. Denton carries a sword; he and Elizabeth fight for their lives against the savage dogs of the Food Company. For a weapon, she finds a rusting spade.

> It might have been the first century instead of the twenty-second,
> so far as she was concerned. All the gentleness of her eighteen
> years of city life vanished before this primordial need.[46]

With the spade, she cleaves a wild dog's skull. But civilization
has left them too soft for country life; they are forced back into
the city, where they anticipate and spend a legacy of Elizabeth's.
As a last desperate resort, they are forced to go to the Labour
Company, which, though it was originally a charitable organization, now holds a third of the people of the world as "its serfs
and debtors from the cradle to the grave."

In the people of the lower levels, as in the Morlocks of *The
Time Machine*, there is evidence that Wells did not like or understand the urban proletariat as well as he did the rural folk of
southern England. Neither democrat nor Marxist, he was afraid of
the common man. Bergonzi quotes a Marxist critic:

> That fear remained with Wells all his life. He might pity the work-
> ers, he might want to brighten their lives, but he could never see
> them as anything but a destructive force which must be led and
> controlled and, if necessary, coerced.[47]

As Wells saw the process of social evolution, it would tend to
isolate and alienate all kinds of special groups. He shows this
tendency separating the Morlocks and the Eloi in *The Time Machine*, and he projects it to an ultimate conclusion in *The First
Men in the Moon*.

In only two centuries, the barriers between the upper classes
and the wearers of the blue canvas have risen so high that Denton and Elizabeth, among the labor serfs, feel almost as if they
were falling among inferior animals.[48] Yet Wells sees a kind of
ambiguous virtue in the primitive side of life in the depths. In a
passage that recalls Jack London, Denton is befriended by one
decent wearer of the blue, who fights him, defends him from the
bullies, and instructs him in self-defense.

The same kind of ambiguity is reflected in Denton's attitudes
toward social progress. In an hour of depression, he sees civilization as "a monstrous fraud . . . a vast lunatic growth, producing a deepening torrent of savagery below, and above ever more
flimsy gentility and silly wastefulness." He perceives civilization "as some catastrophic product as little concerned with men—
save as victims—as a cyclone or a planetary collision."[49] But
this gloomy view of society is suddenly brightened when his
newly learned primitive skills enable him to defeat the bully.
"The idea that he was a martyr in the civilisation machine had

vanished from his mind. He was now a man in the world of men."[50] In this more expansive mood, he has a vision of progress as the growth of

> a Being of Life in which we live and move and have our being, something that began fifty—a hundred million years ago, perhaps, that goes on—on: growing, spreading, to things beyond us, things that will justify us all.

His bruises and his pain become "the chisel of the Maker."[51]

Despite a few such optimistic instants, however, the world of Ugh-lomi seems far preferable to that of Denton and Elizabeth: all the centuries of progress have resulted in a net decline. Ugh-lomi and his mate fight bloodily but successfully for survival and mastery of the squatting place. Denton and Elizabeth strive in vain against the devouring society of the future. They are saved not through any effort or merit of their own, nor even through any beneficent consequence of fifty thousand years of social advancement. They are rescued instead by the author, by means of an unconvincing *deus ex machina*: the playboy Bindon, overtaken with the wages of his life in the Pleasure Cities, suddenly requests Euthanasia and leaves Elizabeth his heir.

The story closes with a vision of creative evolution—seen not as any obscure metaphysical influence, but as a practical result of accumulating scientific knowledge. Bindon's optimistic young doctor foresees a time when science will assume the management of society.

> Some of us have a sort of fancy that in time we may know enough to take over a little more than the ventilation and the drains. Knowledge keeps on piling up, you know. It keeps on growing. . . . Some day, men will live in a different way.[52]

Both novelettes, in summary, present optimistic visions of progress somewhat dimmed by romantic yearnings for the primitive past. In neither story does Wells succeed in making a dramatic asset of his own divided attitudes, as he does with Graham and Ostrog in *When the Sleeper Wakes* and with Bedford and Cavor in *The First Men in the Moon*. Both stories are exercises in intellectual speculation, and consequently lack the richly imagined and complex symbolism of his best work. Yet Wells, with his wealth of ideas, his splashes of vivid color, and his melodramatic action, has made both stories highly readable. Even though he is writing in praise of progress, on his ambivalent balances the appeal of the past seems to outweigh the promise of the future.

3 When the Sleeper Wakes

The future world of *The Time Machine* is, as Wells writes in the autobiography, "a mere fantasy based on the idea of the human species developing about divergent lines."[53] In *When the Sleeper Wakes*,[54] he is making a more systematic study of the trends of progress, in greater detail and nearer at hand. His method of extrapolation from the present to the future is outlined in *The Future in America*: "one sets to work to trace the great changes of the last century or so, and one produces these on a straight line and according to the rule of three."[55] The plot pattern is borrowed from Bellamy's *Looking Backward* (1888), whose hero "had so oddly anticipated this actual experience" (Ch. 7). Bellamy, however, was writing a didactic utopia of the world as he wanted to make it; Wells, in the better part of his book, is offering a realistic social forecast of a future he dreads. This novel, however, is flawed by Wells' conflicting attitudes.

The evidence hints that he did not understand the trouble. He calls the book "one of the most ambitious and least satisfactory" of his earlier novels,[56] and admits that he "scamped the finish" of it in his haste to leave for Italy on a trip with Jane,[57] because *Love and Mr. Lewisham*, which he was writing at the same time, had "taken a very much stronger hold" upon his affections.[58] He writes Bennett, "There's good stuff in it, but it's a big confused disintegrating thing."[59] In one letter to Gissing he shows his early elation when the story had "assumed really noble proportions,"[60] and in another letter his later frustration: "I'm having awful times with my beggar. He won't shape. . . . I'm midway between a noble performance and a noble disaster."[61] Dissatisfied with the novel, he undertook to revise it for a new edition which finally appeared in 1910 with a few changes and a few thousand words omitted.[62] The generally unfavorable critical reception[63] may have contributed to the decision which he announced in *Anticipations* that fiction and prophecy do not mix.[64]

When the Sleeper Wakes lacks the unity and power of the best of the scientific fantasies, perhaps because Wells' systematic method of social prophecy had left him too close to his material. The earlier romances, as Bergonzi points out, had been mythical and symbolic.[65] Although Wells' new method of projecting the probable future does not create a world of symbolic myth, it does act as a powerful magnifier for the actual forces of social change. In the words of Anthony West, the book

is the nightmare of a man who would have liked to find himself inside Shelley's imagination but finds himself instead inside Hobbes'; and its most frightening aspect is that the tyranny it describes is not just a construction with an ideological basis, but an organic growth. It has evolved from the society of 1899 along lines set by the weaknesses of the average man and woman, and is simply a machine for expoliting those weaknesses to the utmost.

West concludes that the novel shows Wells' fundamental pessimism more clearly than even *The Island of Dr. Moreau*, and that it "makes one realize how far his later optimism went against the native grain of his thought."[66]

Bergonzi suggests that the book is incoherent, partly because of the unsatisfactory mixture of prophecy and fiction, partly because of a fatigued imagination, and more largely because of the conflicting ambiguities of Wells' imaginative and intellectual attitudes. In the earlier fiction, Wells had been able to express his "dual allegiance both to the past and the future" in terms of imaginative symbolism,

> but from about 1898 onward Wells' concern with the future was to be expressed in increasingly intellectual terms and his imagination became increasingly coerced by his intellectual convictions.[67]

The later Wells, in other words, was trying to impose upon himself an intellectual discipline that violated some of his most profound emotional attitudes.

Wells describes his projection of the social background for the novel as

> essentially an exaggeration of contemporary tendencies: higher buildings, bigger towns, wickeder capitalists and labour more down-trodden than ever and more desperate. . . . It was our contemporary world in a state of highly inflamed distension.[68]

The hero, Graham, is one side of Wells himself: the Wells who cherished an idealistic hope for human progress. "A man of considerable gifts, but spasmodic, emotional." So another character describes him.

> He had grave domestic troubles, divorced his wife in fact. . . . He was a fanatical Radical—a Socialist—or typical Liberal, as they used to call themselves, of the advanced school (Ch. 2).

He has written a controversial pamphlet of social prophecy that was "wild, whirling stuff." At the beginning of the novel, he falls asleep. When he wakes, after two centuries, he finds that the accumulated income from certain unearned legacies has made him the nominal owner of half the earth—a development perhaps intended to satirize capitalism. The actual power is vested in a council of trustees, who have used this snowballing wealth to establish a tyranny of property which mercilessly expolits "a third of the people." His awakening is used to arouse the blue-clad masses against the council. Graham attempts to aid the revolt until he discovers that its leader, Ostrog, is planning to betray the people. Resisting Ostrog, he dies fighting to defend the insurgent masses from an air fleet that is bringing Negro troops to put them down.

Even today, most of a turbulent century after it was written, *When the Sleeper Wakes* is still impressive as a novel of scientific and social prophecy. History has lagged behind the forecasts in some directions, and run ahead in others; Wells says nothing here about space flight or atomic energy, but his roofed city with its moving streets and cableways is still strange enough to evoke the sense of wonder. Time has not always chosen the Wellsian nomenclature: our electronic communication systems are not called Babble Machines, or even General Intelligence Machines, but they are used in the same way for broadcasting commercial and political propaganda. If the people of a few favored Western nations seem happier than Wells predicted, we may either reflect that his forecast period has another hundred and thirty years to go, or look at the rest of the world. Though Wells was writing before the Wright brothers flew at Kitty Hawk, his descriptions of air travel and air battles are convincing and exciting. He not only conveys the sensations of flight, but anticipates the tactics and strategy of air warfare. He has caught the heartless power of the labor racketeer, the nauseating intimacy of the television commercial, the sex freedom of the commune, the monopolistic self-interest of the American Medical Association, and the commercialized religion that offers "Brisk Blessings for Busy Business Men" (Ch. 20).

Graham is awed by the technological progress he finds, but astonished to see how little it has done for common men. Life and property are secure over most of the world, diseases have been conquered, people are adequately fed and clothed, "but the crowd . . . was a crowd still, helpless in the hands of demogogue and organiser, individually cowardly, individually swayed by appetite, collectively incalculable" (Ch. 14).

Aided only by an idealistic girl, Graham is powerless to alter the trends toward centralization and specialization manifest in Ostrog. Through most of the book he is a somewhat shadowy figure, a mere spectator appalled by this world of unrestrained materialism. A rather wooden symbol of an anachronistic ideal of progress, he finds abundant evidence of social evolution but no realization of his idealistic hopes. The rich are as useless as the childish Eloi. In a gallery of prominent people, Wells introduces an "amorist," a fashionable "capillotomist," the "Black Labor Master," a bishop and one of his "subsidiary wives," an educator who boasts of having "completely conquered Cram," and the charming daughter of the manager of the Piggeries of the European Food Trust (Ch. 15). These people are fantastically conspicuous consumers; they waste their lives at Pleasure Cities, employ hypnotists to remove unhappiness, and finally ask for the expensive rites of Euthanasy. They represent the corruption and destruction of the individual self.

The poor have been forced into the Labour Company. Their women are flat-chested and plain, because the more attractive have been weeded out by the Pleasure Cities and the Euthanasia clinics through centuries of natural selection. They are all pinched and feeble; the burly worker of Victorian times has followed the draft horse into extinction. They send their unwanted infants to the mechanized crèches, and bow to the black police. As a follower of Darwin and Huxley, Wells feels that the evolutionary process will wipe out the unfit—who, in this age of ever more narrow specialization, are the unskilled, the unspecialized.

Although the novel has been remarkably influential,[69] it does have real faults. Like "A Story of the Days to Come," it contains more intellectual speculation than fully imagined symbolic action. The first half of the book is weak in narrative interest; here Graham is merely a bewildered spectator, not a participant. The original ending makes him a melodramatic hero: having learned to pilot a small aircraft, he goes up alone to defeat the whole air armada that is bringing Negro troops to crush the movement for freedom. (He dies in the revised version too, but is uncertain of his victory.)

Weak and isolated as he is, however, Graham does function as an effective symbol of the relativity of progress. He is the selfless social man, bewildered to discover that social evolution has left him behind. His quarrel with Ostrog reflects Wells' conflict with himself. Graham represents Wells' own growing hope for progress toward a world where "all men and women might live nobly, in freedom and peace" (Ch. 23). But every feature of the future world reveals Wells' scientific certainty that progress is more likely to destroy the free individual than to create the utopia he longs for.

Though the ambiguous ending does show Wells' deep reluctance to accept his own pessimistic intellectual conclusions, the strongest theme of the book is the relative and ambivalent nature of progress. Exploring the forces shaping the future, Wells finds no support for his idealistic hopes, but instead the ugly outlines of all the totalitarian dictatorships that have flourished since he wrote. Progress as adaptation for survival is as inevitable as the accumulation of knowledge, but the sort of progress Wells and Graham wanted, progress toward the liberation of the human spirit, is at best no more than an uncertain alternative to universal slavery and destruction, a possible but unlikely reward for intelligence and courage and compassionate effort. It must reckon forever with Ostrog.

Ostrog, in contrast to Graham, is the animal man, the selfish primitive intellect. As another side of Wells, he is the scientific realist. As prophecy, he prefigures Krushchev and Hitler and Peron and De Gaulle, and doubtless other Overmen yet to appear. Like the Grand Lunar in *The First Men in the Moon* and like Wells himself, he views democracy with contempt. Cynically, in his own push for power he has used "the old ideals of universal happiness—all men equal—all men happy" (Ch. 19). Now in power, because he has the air "and the mastery of the air is the mastery of the earth," he assures Graham coolly that social evolution has now discarded democracy in favor of aristocratic tyranny.

> It is the way that change has always travelled. Aristocracy, the prevalence of the best—suffering and extinction for the unfit, and so to better things. . . . The Crowd is a huge foolish beast.

Ostrog in his boyhood had "read your Shelley and dreamt of liberty," but now he says "there is no liberty, save in wisdom and self-control." So long as nature breeds sheep, he will be among the beasts of prey.

Through a bitter paradox, Ostrog's selfish drive for power and Graham's idealistic self-abnegation operate in parallel. Ostrog would destroy the individual rights of all except himself; Graham urges individual surrender to "an immortal life of Humanity in which we live and move and have our being" (Ch. 23). Both are aiding the evolution of a more rigid social order, in which individual liberty must fade and die. This is the main trend of change revealed by Wells' method of extrapolating the future. The progressive idealism of the nineteenth century had been merely an eddy in the stream of thought.

4 The First Men in the Moon

The basic ambiguity of Wells' view of progress shows up clearly in *The First Men in the Moon*.[70] The book is often read simply as a great space adventure story used as a vehicle for incidental satire on human specialization.[71] Kingsley Amis writes that "Wells's main drive here is simple delight in invention, in working out an alien ecology, typical of what I might call primitive science fiction."[72] Norman Nicholson, although he gives Wells credit for basing a romantic myth upon everyday life and brilliantly investing it with the sense of wonder and even for "satirising to some extent," yet says that "on the whole he is just improvising for the sheer joy of it."[73] Basil Davenport classifies *The First Men in the Moon*, along with *The Time Machine*, among the "utopias in reverse, showing the degeneration of a society."[74] As Wells states his own purpose, he intended "to look at mankind from a distance and burlesque the effects of specialization."[75] His actual accomplishment is greater and more complex than such comments suggest, even though somewhat weakened by his own ambivalent attitudes.

It is the last of Wells' great fantastic romances, and, in his own opinion, probably the best.[76] As a sustained effort of creative imagination, it has seldom been equalled. Wells came to the story from the two or three years of analytic study of human progress that had produced *Anticipations*[77] and *When the Sleeper Wakes*. Perhaps the act of writing this novel helped to bring some of his internal conflicts into conscious reconciliation. After *The First Men in the Moon*, at any rate, they seem to subside. They flare up briefly again, in a few such stories as "The Country of the Blind." But the later scientific romances, *The Food of the Gods* (1904) and *In the Days of the Comet* (1906)[78] and the rest, lack the concrete reality and the sustained dramatic interest of the earlier stories, perhaps because that inner drive had ceased to operate.

The First Men in the Moon is less original in outline than most of the earlier scientific novels, which are generally shaped by Wells' own ideas in collision. Here he deliberately follows an old conventional form, the imaginary voyage,[79] as he acknowledges with the epigraph from Lucien's *Icaromenippus*. Many details of plot and setting are borrowed from the traditions of the *genre*. The plant life of the moon, gigantic in size and brief in span of life, comes from Kepler's *Somnium*.[80] The freedom of the space voyagers from hunger and thirst and fatigue, which are seen as effects of gravity, follows Francis Godwin's *Manne in the Moone: or a Discourse on a Voyage Thither by Domingo Gonzales*, published in 1638.[81] The gold so abundant in the moon is borrowed from *A Voyage to Cacklogallinia* (1727) by "Captain Samuel Brunt,"[82] a satire on the South Sea Bubble.

Wells found most of the details of his moon ship in more recent stories of the same *genre*. The shape and equipment of the craft echo Jules Verne's hollow cannon ball in *De la Terre a la Lune* (1865). The Cavorite used to lift it is anticipated by *Lunarium*, a new metal that is repelled instead of being attracted by the earth in *A Voyage to the Moon: with some account of the Manners and Customs, Science and Philosophy, of the People of Morosufia and other Lunarians* (pseudonymous, 1827),[83] and also by Apergy, a repulsive force used to drive the immense space ship in Percey Gregg's *Across the Zodiac* (1880).[84] The accidental loss of the ship after Bedford's return to earth comes from Hugh McColl's *Mr. Stranger's Sealed Packet* (1889), in which precisely the same kind of accident sends Mr. Stranger's ship, the Shooting Star, off into space after his return to earth, with his meddlesome landlady and her daughter screaming inside the open door.[85]

Though his plot is not entirely new, Wells presents it with an imaginative and narrative power far ahead of his originals. For a striking contrast, he begins his tale "of super-terrestial and aerial topics" with his characters mired in very convincing adhesive mud at Lympne, at the edge of Romney marsh, in the clay part of Kent. The narrator, Bedford, is an undischarged bankrupt, rusticating while he writes a play that he hopes will restore his losses. He meets Cavor, who is perfecting his gravity screen, and they are soon landing the Cavorite sphere on the moon—just in time to watch the daily thawing of the frozen air and the explosive growth of the lunar jungle. Lost from the sphere, they are captured by Selenites that have come out to pasture moon-calves. They are carried into the moon. Bedford leads an escape, finds the sphere, and gets back to earth with a fortune in golden chains and crowbars. Cavor is left in the moon. His further adventures are revealed through a series of wireless messages. Recaptured, Cavor has been taken deep into the lunar hive, where he observes the physical and social adaptations that fit each Selenite for his own place in an utterly rigid society. When he reveals too much of the selfish destructiveness of mankind, his messages are abruptly cut off.

As sheer thriller, Bedford's story is hard to surpass. Kepler's enormous plants, imagined with the aid of Wells' biological training, help create an unforgettable atmosphere. "The very cells that built up these plants were as large as my thumb, like beads of colored glass" (Ch. 9). Against that background of wonder and hostile mystery, we hear the "Boom . . . Boom . . . Boom . . ." of underground machines, we see the opening of the enormous lid above the shaft, we meet the grotesque herdsmen and their bellowing cattle. Captured, we follow the river of blue light down into the moon, fight our way out through the cave of the moon butchers, find the jungle "brown and sere now and thirty feet high . . . brittle and ready to fall and crumple under the freezing air, so soon as the nightfall came" (Ch. 18). Struggling back to the sphere, Bedford leaps, and each leap is seven ages.

> Before me the pale serpent-girdled sector of the sun sank and sank and the advancing shadow swept to seize the sphere before I could reach it.

Exhausted in the thinning air, he crawls. The frost gathers on his lips, icicles hang from his moustache and beard, he is "white with the freezing atmosphere."

In spite of all this breath-taking verisimilitude, however, Wells is writing not science fiction but his own sort of scientific fantasy. Jules Verne couldn't quite understand it.[86] Actually, in spite of the patter about helium and the circumstantial details of its making and testing, Cavorite is as impossible as travel in time or invisibility; its existence would violate the law of the conservation of energy. Wells' carelessness with bare scientific fact is evident when he lets Bedford write that the moon has "only an eighth part of the earth's mass and a quarter of its diameter" (Ch. 8), getting the mass too great by a factor of ten. He knew that the moon has no atmosphere, and he must have realized that all the changes produced by the thawing of a frozen atmosphere and the growth and decay of heavy vegetation would be clearly visible to telescopes on earth. But such points of fact or logic scarcely matter. Wells' admitted method is to trick his reader "into an unwary concession to some plausible assumption and get on with his story while the illusion holds."[87] The method here is notably successful.

Delighted as Wells may be, however, with his own skill at spinning a tale of exotic adventure, that is not his main interest in *The First Men in the Moon.* If it were, the four chapters relating the further adventures of Cavor inside the moon would be clumsy anticlimax. In fact they make his point. All the freely borrowed plot materials are only a convenient metaphor for what Wells really wants to say. His real subject is physical and social specialization, regarded as a basic device of evolutionary progress. He follows that subject from the first chapter to the last. He examines it with mixed and sometimes conflicting attitudes, but he never lets it go.

This theme, though more original than the cosmic-voyage story in which it is framed, may have come from Huxley, who wrote in 1892 that

> society is possible only upon the condition that the members shall surrender more or less of their individual freedom of action. . . . Thus the progressive evolution of society means increasing restriction of individual freedom in certain directions.[88]

Even the insectile nature of the Selenites may well have been suggested by a passage in Huxley's "Prolegomena" (1894) to "Evolution and Ethics."

> Social organisation is not peculiar to men. Other societies, such as those constituted by bees and ants, have also arisen out of the advantage of cooperation in the struggle for existence.

Competition among the bees is strictly limited, each queen and drone and worker receiving food so that it can perform its function in the economy of the hive.

> Now this society is the direct product of an organic necessity, impelling each member of it to a course of action which tends to the good of the whole. Each bee has its duty and none has any rights.

Huxley remarks that, although an ethical philosopher among the drones might theorize that "an eternal and immutable principle, innate in each bee" is responsible for this selfless devotion to the common good, the biologist familiar with all the stages of evolution between solitary and hive bees finds in it "simply the perfection of an automatic mechanism, hammered out by the blows of the struggle for existence . . . during long ages of constant variation."[89] Huxley even suggests the comparison between human history and that of the hive. "I see no reason to doubt that, at its origin, human society was as much a product of organic necessity as that of the bees."[90]

The moon is a hive of social insects—although Wells compares the Selenites to ants, rather than to bees, the humming of the moon ceases only when the Grand Lunar is about to speak. Like the symbolic creations of Dr. Moreau, the Selenites show the ultimate plasticity of living matter. They demonstrate progress through specialization of form and function, projected to the limits of Wells' imagination. They range in size and dignity from tiny beings that do the work of small electric motors, to the ruling Grand Lunar, whose "brain-case must have measured many yards in diameter" (Ch. 24). Leather-skinned Selenites herd moon-calves; big-brained Selenites remember facts; siren-voiced Selenites screech orders and information; bellows-lunged Selenites blow glass: "every one of these common Selenites is exquisitely adapted to the social need it meets" (Ch. 23).

As satire upon existing human society, all this is deadly enough. Wells casts human vice or folly into these insect shapes to make it absurd or horrible; then, before we can recoil, he reminds us that this insectile nightmare is more rational and more humane than human society. Cavor is horrified when he sees a method of producing machine-minding specialists: baby Selenites are confined in jars, with one hand protruding to be "stimulated by irritants and nourished by injection while the rest of the body is starved" (Ch. 23). For all his intellectual admiration of "this wonderful social order," Cavor admits that this

> wretched-looking hand sticking out of its jar seemed to me to appeal for lost possibilities; it haunts me still, although, of course, it is really in the end a far more humane proceeding than our earthly method of leaving children to grow into human beings, and then making machines of them.

(The image of this bottled baby must have haunted Aldous Huxley, too; the hive of the Selenites contains many striking anticipations of *Brave New World*.)

Gulliver's adventure with the Houyhnhnms seems to have been the model for Wells' satire here—he often admitted his debt to Swift.[91] His Selenites are as rational as Swift's horses, and his satire, like Swift's, operates at several levels. Satire must attack from a base upon some accepted norm. Man, as Cavor reveals him to the Grand Lunar, no more fits the rational norm of the Selenites than does man, revealed by Gulliver to his master, fit the norm of the superior horses. Yet that rational norm fails in each case to fit a higher ideal norm. Wells, no more than Swift, intends to praise pure reason. The Grand Lunar is deliberately made pathetic and absurd. He sits in solitary splendor, with attendants spraying cooling fluids over his distended brain. "Ineffectual-looking little hand-tentales steadied this shape on the throne. . . . It was great. It was pitiful" (Ch. 24).

However devastating, this burlesque upon specialization in contemporary society is only a minor part of Wells' main theme.

His elaborate construction of the lunar culture is a very serious study of the division of labor as a tendency of progress. The ant-like Selenites, with their rigid social organization and their complex physical adaptations, are a logical culmination of the kind of progress that began in the seas of ancient earth when the first groups of sister cells began to cooperate instead of simply competing for survival. Effective enough as a satiric image of modern mankind, the Selenites are at the same time seriously prophetic of man's probable future: a future which Wells examines with deeply divided feelings. Sometimes his fascination with the rational world order of the moon is pure admiration, but more often it slips into something nearer horror. In writing the story, Wells seems to be proving to himself that the selfless conformity of the Selenites is the only ultimate alternative to such selfish human disorders as greed and war, but he shrinks from both horns of the dilemma.

Bedford in the novel is the unspecialized individual, resisting the law of the hive. Unmarried and unattached, he is waging a solitary war both against human society on earth and against its satiric symbol in the moon. Lacking special adaptations, he is ready for anything but competent at nothing except the most primitive sort of cunning and slaughter. He has failed in business. We find him writing a play, with no special training and no visible prospect of success. He gets lost on the moon, gets drunk on lunar mushrooms, gets himself and Cavor captured. He is too primitive to understand the rational Selenites. After his escape, he sleeps on his way to search for the sphere and fails to signal Cavor after he has found it. Back on earth, he leaves the moon ship open to trap a meddling boy.

His one spectacular success is the triumph of his brute strength over the civilized Selenites. When he strikes the first one with the golden chain wrapped around his fist, the moon creature

> smashed like some sort of sweetmeat with liquid in it. He broke right in. He squelched and splashed. It was like hitting a damp toadstool. The flimsy body went spinning a dozen yards and fell with a flabby impact (Ch. 14).

His primitive strength snaps chains and bends bars. A man berserk, he massacres his Selenite pursuers.

> I remember . . . wading among these leathery thin things as a man wades through tall grass, mowing and hitting, first right then left—smash, smash! . . . It did not seem to me that the Selenites were unexpectedly flimsy, but that I was unexpectedly strong. I laughed stupidly (Ch. 16).

This display of selfish primitive violence as the invulnerable enemy of civilized society is an important link in the symbolism.

Bedford is as purely selfish, at the beginning, as the Invisible Man. When he first hears of Cavorite, it strikes him as

> one of those chances that come once in a thousand years. . . .
> Among other things, I saw in it my redemption as a business
> man. . . . "We're on absolutely the biggest thing that has ever
> been invented," I said, and put the accent on "we" (Ch. 1).

When he finds gold in the moon, "knocking about like cast iron at home," he immediately determines to come back "in a bigger sphere with guns" (Ch. 15). Although he claims extenuating circumstances, his own selfishness aids Cavor's recapture by the Selenites. His narrow concentration on his own immediate comfort allows Master Tommy Simmons to trap himself in the unguarded sphere.

He is no villain, however, for all his naked selfishness, but rather a comic hero. His candid confessions strike the universal human chord of self. He is acceptable because his selfish behavior is generally shortsighted and unsuccessful. He has been the victim of malignant creditors, and his adventures satirize the collective selfishness of society. His own primal selfishness is relieved, as the story goes on, by flashes of concern for Cavor. Alone in space after he has left Cavor behind on the moon, he sees a new view of himself.

> The most prominent quality of it was a pervading doubt of my own
> identity. . . . I saw Bedford in many relations. . . . I saw him not
> only as an ass, but as the son of many generations of asses (Ch.
> 19).

Back on earth, however, he is soon himself again. Prudently changing his name to protect the gold from his creditors, he publishes his narrative as fiction under the name of "Wells" (Ch. 20).

In contrast to Bedford, Cavor is the specialist and therefore the social man. As specialized intelligence, he is the human counterpart of the Grand Lunar. Yet he seeks no personal advantage through his intellect; as scientist, he is the polar opposite of the self-seeking Invisible Man. Lacking the essential human traits of self, Cavor has the nature of a machine. "A short, round-bodied, thin-legged little man, with a jerky quality in his motions," he first appears walking by Bedford's house, gesticulating and jerking his head about and buzzing "like something electric." He stops, looks at his watch, turns convulsively back toward his laboratory. Like a marionette, he repeats this same mechanical behavior every evening at the same time in the same way, until Bedford makes him helpless by breaking his set pattern of habit.

His only passion is knowledge. Utterly selfless, he is as indifferent to the practical uses of Cavorite as he is to the accidental damage caused by his first experiment with it, which comes near whipping the atmosphere off the earth "as one peels a banana." To Bedford's astonishment, he has "troubled no more about the stuff he was going to turn out than if he had been a machine to make guns" (Ch. 2). As Bedford points out, he has never married, never grown richer than he happened to be; he has just "rooted after knowledge" (Ch. 15). He conceals his responsibility for the disaster at Lympne because he "cannot consent for one moment to add the burden of practical considerations to [his] theorizing" (Ch. 2). Even as the prisoner of the Selenites, as Bedford says,

> He was not absolutely in despair at the prospect of going ever deeper into this inhuman planet burrow. His mind ran on machines and invention to the exclusion of a thousand dark things that beset me. It wasn't that he intended to make any use of these things: he simply wanted to know them (Ch. 14).

Cavor is appalled by Bedford's violent resistance to the Selenites, horrified by Bedford's intention of coming back with guns. The man of reason against the man of instinct, in the messages from the moon he accuses Bedford of becoming "impulsive, rash, and quarrelsome," and of making off with the sphere in order to "steal a march" on him. In his audience with the Grand Lunar, however, he is betrayed by what Bedford calls "his disastrous want of vulgar common sense" (Ch. 25). The Selenites learn about men, and learn that he alone knows the secret of making Cavorite. Rationally, they stop his messages before he can transmit the information that might bring Bedford back to loot the moon.

Cavor's austere intellectuality is warmed by occasional human inconsistencies. Sometimes he shows a flash of liking for Bedford. Though his education has been "purely scientific," he carries the works of Shakespeare with him to the moon. His intellectual admiration for the wonderful social organization of the Selenites is tempered at times by aversion or horror. At the end of the novel, in spite of his acceptance of the rational ideals of universal peace and order symbolized by the Selenites, he dies fighting for survival.

The novel is alive because of the dramatic tension between two attitudes in Wells himself. Cavor is the social man, the enlightened intellectual, pointing the way to progress through an ever more elaborate division of labor. Bedford is the animal man, the primitive ego, denying the biological law that reads: specialize or die. Wells himself wavers between the two. He clearly disapproves of the brutal greed that would make Bedford a second Pizarro. He sees with Cavor and the Grand Lunar the need of a social structure strong enough to end war and waste and to control the human environment. But, doubting that the brain is an instrument of virtue, Wells is not content with rational conclusions. Anthony West writes:

> What Wells is saying here is that a further extension of human intellectual powers in the post-Renaissance direction of abstract rational thinking will lead to the growth of cruel and inhuman planned societies utterly indifferent to individuals and individual happiness. The scientific apparatus for examining reality is hostile to values since it shows that any system of values is purely arbitrary.[92]

Progress, to Wells the biologist, is simply the resultant of a ceaseless series of improvised efforts to survive. The life of the novel grows from the hopeless struggle of Wells the artist to deny that fact.

Bedford and Cavor can, of course, be explored from other points of view; a psychiatrist would doubtless analyze them in another language altogether. The warrant for treating them as symbols for Wells' own competing egoistic and social selves comes in the first place from my own long experience at projecting private emotions into fictional characters. The vindication of this approach comes from all it reveals of Wells' mind and work.

In *The First Men in the Moon*, Wells is examining specialization and particularly intellectual specialization as a source of future progress. Using the evolutionary history of the social insects as a guide, he projects it to infinity. As a scientist, he can visualize adaptations that will make the human race more efficient. As a human being, he is horrified by what he sees. In the outcome, Cavor is betrayed and destroyed by his own intellect. Bedford is saved by his undisciplined individualism. Wells himself, torn between these conflicting attitudes, seems at last to indicate a choice when he lets Bedford borrow his own name for a by-line.

In Another Century

1 The Prophet of Progress, 1901-1946

The whole story of H. G. Wells has not yet been told. Gordon Ray was once at work on a definitive life and letters, based on the papers in the Wells Archive at the University of Illinois, but this has not appeared. The task is enormous. Wells was active for another forty-five years after he finished *The First Men in the Moon*. He wrote fine comic novels in *Kipps* (1905) and *Tono-Bungay* (1909) and *The History of Mr. Polly* (1910). He was variously fond husband and free lover, hack writer and inspiring teacher, spokesman for his generation and citizen of the world, utopian philosopher and eloquent prophet of his own brand of progress.

The literary and journalistic output of those busy decades is too vast to be surveyed here, but a glance at *A Modern Utopia*[1] will show the shift in his thought. Though his criticism of progress has changed to evangelism, his underlying attitudes remain remarkably consistent. Perhaps because his own internal struggle has been so largely resolved, his approach is becoming speculative and intellectual, rather than dramatic and emotional, but he is still very much aware of the limitations of the average individual man, whose animal nature has always been the most immediate barrier to progress. His new utopia is carefully built

121

upon his old assumptions that our nature and our environment are both hostile to ideal progress.

> We are to restrict ourselves first to the limitations of human possibility as we know them in the men and women of this world today, and then to all the inhumanity, all the insubordination of nature. We are to shape our state in a world of uncertain seasons, sudden catastrophes, antagonistic diseases, and inimical beasts and vermin, out of men and women with like passions, like uncertainties of mood and desire to our own. And, moreover, we are going to accept this world of conflict, to adopt no attitude of renunciation to it, to face it in no ascetic spirit, but in the mood of the Western peoples, whose purpose is to survive and overcome.[2]

With very much the same technique he had used in the early fiction, Wells plants his utopian premise among these known facts and then examines the necessary consequences. He points out the flaws of the classical utopias, correcting them in the blueprints for his own new state. The earlier utopias have generally been placed on islands or in isolated valleys; he sees that the modern utopia must be a world state. Their energy has commonly come from "the muscular exertion of toiling men,"[3] but Wells recognizes the use and the beauty of machines. Earlier utopians have commonly ignored the inequality of men; in a chapter on failure Wells finds room for social misfits. Most utopias have overlooked the problems of race; in a strong plea for racial understanding, Wells writes, "For my own part I am disposed to discount all adverse judgements and all statements of insurmountable differences between race and race."[4] Considering the status of women, he allows group marriages and advocates state care for children.

His basic premise, consistent enough with his earlier stress on the human limits to progress, is that society can be good. Discussing his scheme for a central index of all citizens, an "inventory of the State [that] would watch its every man," he defends this kind of totalitarian infringement on privacy. To the Liberal,

> brought up to be against the Government on principle, this organized clairvoyance will be the most hateful of dreams. Perhaps, too, the Individualist would see it in that light. But these are only the mental habits acquired in an evil time. The old Liberalism assumed bad government . . . just as it assumed the natural righteousness of the free individual. . . . But suppose we do not assume that government is necessarily bad, and the individual necessarily good . . . then we alter the case altogether."[5]

No democrat, Wells classifies the citizens of utopia into four general types, "The Poietic, the Kinetic, the Dull, and the Base."[6] The first two are "the living tissue of the State." From them he draws the *samuari*, the special class of dedicated and self-disciplined aristocrats who founded the utopia and who rule it now. The Poietic are the imaginative creators, the Kinetic are the able people without much originality. The two types are antagonistic, the Poietic making for growth and the Kinetic for stability. Wells favors the Poietic. Finding "the ultimate significance of life in individuality, novelty and the undefined," the utopians cultivate and reward creative individuality.

The Dull are "the stupid people, the incompetent people . . . who gravitate toward and below the minimum wage that qualifies for marriage. . . . They count neither for work nor direction in the State." Even lower in social value, the Base seem to concentrate all those human qualities that Wells has always found most hazardous to progress.

> The Base have a narrower and more persistent egoistic reference than the common run of humanity; they may boast, but they have no frankness; they have relatively great powers of concealment, and they are capable of, and sometimes have an aptitude and inclination toward, cruelty. In the queer phrasing of earthly psychology with its clumsy avoidance of analysis, they have no "moral sense." They count as an antagonism to the State Organization.[7]

Ill-fitted for survival in utopian society, these lower types are denied power and offspring. Utopia is ruled by the self-elected, creative élite.

The book is transitional in form as well as in thought, showing Wells midway between the literary artist and the propagandist. More essay than novel, it is alive with ideas, but leavened with fictional bits of character, dialog, and plot. Wells is still craftsman enough to achieve his aim, "a sort of shot-silk texture between philosophical discussion on the one hand and imaginative narrative on the other."[8]

Before it appeared, Wells had already earned a world reputation, very largely with the early science fiction. During the first two decades of the new century, as Mark Hillegas says, "he was the great leader of the new generation, an angry young man fighting against the whole of a planless, greedy society."[9] With *A Modern Utopia*, he seemed to win another victory. Its impact was enormous, winning him new admiration from such intellectuals as Henry James, Joseph Conrad, and William James, who said he had "given a shove to the practical thought of the next generation."

Wells devoted most of his energy for the rest of his life to improving and promoting this grandly optimistic plan for the future of the race. He wrote other memorable utopias, such as *Men Like Gods* (1923). Absorbed for a time with improving the status of women and revising the role of sex in society, he wrote a whole series of marriage novels: *Ann Veronica* (1909), *The New Machiavelli* (1911), *Marriage* (1912), *The Passionate Friends* (1913), *The Wife of Sir Isaac Harman* (1914), and *The Research Magnificent* (1915). He invaded politics, attempting to take control of the Fabian Society as a spearhead for his utopian advance. He redefined God and invented a new religion. Seeking to educate the people of the world into fit citizens of the planet, he rewrote history to reveal the evolution of his utopian world state in *The Outline of History* (1920), redefined the potentials and the limits of mankind in *The Science of Life* (1931), and revised the social sciences in *The Work, Wealth, and Happiness of Mankind* (1932).

W. Warren Wagar's *H. G. Wells and the World State* is a brilliant study of this long campaign to realize his magnificent vision. "Everything about Wells' thinking bears the stamp of Utopianism," Wagar writes, "and a balanced picture of his Utopia is impossible without taking all his work into account." Utopias may represent static absolutes, like Plato's Republic or St. Augustine's City of God, "or they may idealize an infinitely self-perfecting and self-transcending society, . . . reflecting Enlightenment and post-Enlightenment ideas of progress through science or the 'laws' of evolution." Wells projected the latter kind. "His Utopias were not strictly ideal societies at all, but rather societies emancipated from the past, ideal in comparison to historic societies, but capable of more or less infinite progress in time."[10]

Summing up Wells' career as prophet of the world state, Wagar suggests that he taught "his serious readers to adjust their thinking to world perspectives." Far ahead of most other men, he perceived the essential fact that the future holds one world or none. "The idea of a world crisis, the writing of world history, the movement for world government, the concept of a world economy, the prophecy of a world Utopia—all have significant origins in his work."[11]

For nearly two decades after *A Modern Utopia*, Wells seemed to be widening a secure beachhead for his boldly planned global society. He held the attention of the world and the respect of intellectuals. He talked to world leaders. Wagar credits him with preparing public opinion for the League of Nations.

His utopian position was always in danger, however, from the same hostility to progress he had dramatized in the early science fiction. A series of defeats eroded his hopes. His attempt to reform the Fabian Society into an effective instrument of social revolution was frustrated by a conservative Old Guard of such traditional literary intellectuals as George Bernard Shaw.[12] Though the liberal notions about love and sex he embodied in *Ann Veronica* and the other marriage novels may now seem quaintly out of date, they were then new enough to shock critics, alienate readers, and make trouble with his publisher.[13] His utopian religion of deified man found few converts. The savage carnage of World War I was a stunning blow to all utopian optimism, and the history of the socialist states that arose in its wake was grim enough to blight most of the surviving faith in man's ability to redesign his world. Wells was left almost alone on his battered beachhead, ignored by the younger generation and abandoned by the intellectuals. Though he carried on the fight to the end of his life (on the afternoon of August 13, 1946), he lived his last years in the bitter role of the prophet scorned, all his warnings ignored.

2   Wells and the Two Cultures

When we consider the wide and eager support Wells found at the dawn of the century for his stirring pleas of progress toward a utopian world community, when we feel the disquieting shadow of his foreseen Armageddon lying over our divided world today, the loss of his influential early followers calls for explanation. This alienation of the intellectuals is best explained, I believe, by Sir Charles Snow's notion that our world is torn between two cultures, the scientific and the traditional, each blind to the values of the other.[14]

Older than Snow, this tragic quarrel involved Wells all his life. Tradition ruled his childhood, manifest in his mother's religion and all the folkways of her social class. Reading *Gulliver* in the library at Up Park, he must have been impressed by the force of Swift's attacks on uncontrolled reason and misapplied science. On the other side, his own great teacher, T. H. Huxley, had defended scientific education with the lecture "Science and Culture" in 1881–to which Matthew Arnold had replied in 1882 with his Rede Lecture at Cambridge, "Science and Literature." Reading the early fiction, we can trace the same struggle in the mind of Wells himself, where the culture of science won a slow and painful victory, never quite complete.

In private life, Wells and George Gissing repeated the Huxley-Arnold debate.[15] The two men were alike in many ways. Both had risen through harsh poverty from the lower middle class, both had broken with religion and turned to socialism, both had known sex frustration and unhappy marriage, both had tried teaching and turned to literature. Yet, in their final attitudes toward life and art, they differed profoundly. Gissing scornfully declined the sort of journalistic opportunity that Wells so readily grasped,[16] and he was destroyed by the same misfortunes in health, love, and marriage that gave such ironic aid to Wells' success. A literary intellectual, Gissing writes in *The Private Papers of Henry Ryecroft* (1903):

> I hate and fear "science" because of my conviction that for long to come, if not forever, it will be the remorseless enemy of mankind. I see it destroying all simplicity and gentleness of life, all the beauty of the world; I see it restoring barbarism under a mask of civilization; I see it darkening men's minds and hardening their hearts; I see it bringing a time of vast conflicts which will pale into insignificance "the thousand wars of old," and as likely as not, will whelm all the laborious advances of mankind in blood-drenched chaos.[17]

The two first met late in 1896, the year Wells published *The Island of Dr. Moreau*. With Gissing as a guide, Wells and his wife toured Rome in 1898. Wells went to visit the dying Gissing in the Pyrenees in 1903. By that date, Wells had passed the climax of his own psychological conflict, and had already turned to new literary *genres* with *Love and Mr. Lewisham* (1900) and *Anticipations* (1901). In the autobiography, he writes of Gissing from a viewpoint in the culture of science:

> At the back of my mind I thought him horribly mis-educated and he hardly troubled to hide from me his opinion that I was abso--lutely illiterate. Each of us had his secret amusement in the other's company. He knew the Greek epics and plays to a level of frequent quotation but I think he took his classical philosophers as read and their finality for granted; he assumed that modern science and thought were merely degenerate recapitulations of their lofty and inaccessible wisdom. . . . He thought that a classical scholar need only turn over a few books to master all that scientific work and modern philosophy had made of the world, and it did not disillusion him in the least that he had no mastery of himself or any living fact in existence. . . .

> Through Gissing I was confirmed in my suspicion that this orthodox classical training which was once so powerful an

antiseptic against Egyptian dogma and natural superstition . . .
has become a vast collection of monumental masonry, a pale
cemetery in a twilight, through which new conceptions hurry
apologetically on their way to town, finding neither home nor
sustenance there. . . . It has ceased to be a field of education
and become a proper hunting ground for the archeologist and
social psychologist.[18]

The lives of both Wells and Gissing illuminate the deeper and
more private battle of self against society, which this debate
reflects. The rebel spirit of the individualist was strong in both
men; neither yielded easily to social compulsions. Wells, however, perhaps because he had formed a more accurate image of
reality, adapted more readily than did Gissing, who remained the
unregenerate egoist to the end. Wells got on with people. He kept
the affections of his parents and brothers. He was able to end
his unfortunate first marriage without much bitterness, and to
conduct his extramarital affairs without losing his second wife.
He got on with his work in much the same way. As Gettmann puts
it, "Wells did not have to come to terms with journalism: he
positively welcomed it."[19] He writes in the autobiography how
he learned from a book of Barrie's how to lower his aim "—and
hit."[20] Unlike Gissing, he was willing all his life to lower his
aim enough to hit. To the literary intellectual, who is likely to
be an unreconstructed individualist, this willingness is read as
lack of artistic integrity. It accounts partly for the disagreement
with Henry James, and perhaps largely for the long eclipse of
Wells' literary reputation.

Wells must have come far toward the resolution of his own
conflict before he began to write. The psychic tensions can only
be inferred, but their traces in the early fiction seem to reveal
stages in the evolution of a social mind. Creating an invading
Martian or a predacious Invisible Man or a machine-like Cavor,
Wells is not so often grappling with his problems of the moment
as finding effective metaphors for simpler and deeper and older
conflicts. Such a reading of the early fiction shows the ghosts of
his private past finding expression and reconciliation, leaving
Wells a mature social man.

A double irony is involved. On the one hand, using fiction to
discharge the buried emotions at odds with his role in society,
Wells earned an individual freedom of thought and behavior that
the uncompromising Gissing never enjoyed. On the other hand—
because, as Yeats puts it, a man's quarrels with himself are the
stuff of poetry—the laying of those ghosts shut off the main
source of his literary power. At least he was left unbound by the

egocentric literary aspirations that hobbled Gissing, free to devote his life to his long campaign for progress. The social man at last, his searching criticism of progress completed, Wells became the champion of his generation for the culture of science.

His personal decision, however, was not the end of the great debate—nor can it end, for this is not the sort of problem that discussion can solve. Rather, the issue serves as an intellectual sieve, which separates unlike temperaments. To those whose values are absolute, even unconsciously, what was best in Homeric Greece is still the best. To those who accept the relativity of culture, what is best is what best serves each new generation. The first group would honor the same commandments forever. The second can understand that "Thou shalt kill" has become the essential ethical commandment of the Morlocks in their symbiotic life with the Eloi.

Sir Charles Snow has now assumed the role of the later Wells, speaking for the culture of science. F. R. Leavis and others have attacked him, with none of Matthew Arnold's friendly restraint. Lionel Trilling, on the side of literature, has attempted to question "the whole concept of culture."[21]

Support for that concept, however, and especially for the pivotal idea of cultural relativity, comes from a theory of culture advanced by the anthropologist Edward T. Hall. Working with the aid of George L. Trager, the linguist, Hall treats culture as "a form of communication."[22] It is communicated on three levels: formal, informal, and technical. The formal aspects of culture are extremely resistant to change, the informal aspects more flexible, the technical aspects often open to change. Hall presents a theory of progress, from formal belief to informal adaptation to technical analysis.[23] No more than Wells, however, does he discover any cultural absolutes. "Man alters experience by living it. There is no experience independent of culture against which culture can be measured.[24]

The new acceleration of change is the fact of life for which the strictly literary intellectual is most painfully unprepared. The world is not only changing, but the rate of change is climbing. In the past, one kind of flaked stone tool might remain in use for a few thousand years. Today, automation every year leaves hundreds of industrial skills obsolete and millions unemployed; the population explosion is bursting the old fabric of society; the very survival of mankind is threatened by weapons unknown a generation ago; we are suddenly drowning in our own pollution. The sort of mind that deliberately ignores the predictable results of technological change seems both socially dangerous and intellectually retarded.

Although Hall's theory adds no new facts, it does suggest that the "conflict of the two cultures" might more accurately be regarded as the discontinuity between the formal and technical levels of one culture. The purely literary scholar, absorbed with the formal modes of the past, tends to accept the formal aspects of his own culture. The physical scientist, working with technical processes, is often forced to challenge the formal part of culture. Since technical behavior often initiates change, the scientist tends to feel that he is taking part in progress. Since change threatens tradition, the literary scholar tends to disapprove of progress and to condemn its Wellsian prophets.

Such generalizations must be used, of course, with caution, because the typical scientist and the typical literary intellectual do not in fact exist. Each individual scholar is a unique human being, functioning at all three cultural levels. Yet the analysis may help to show the motives behind the great debate. The predicament of the literary intellectual is that his pre-scientific image of society is inaccurate, so that his efforts to adjust to it can never entirely succeed. Failing to see that change is normal and that values are therefore relative, he attaches himself to a static image of society and seeks his standards in the past. When inevitable processes threaten the transient institutions with which he is identified, he feels that his own identity is in danger. Lacking the relativistic orientation that might have helped him make a more successful adaptation, he has no choice except to display emotional frustration. Thus Wells may have been a happier man than Gissing because he had a more accurate idea of progress.

Wells certainly tended all his life to disregard the formal patterns of behavior, in favor of the informal and the technical. This tendency accounts for such facts of his personal life as his irregular education, his vocational adventures, and his extramarital escapades, and for such features of his career as his disagreement with Henry James, his impatience with the short story as a literary type, and even his campaign for the world state. But that freedom had been laboriously earned, in the long and bitter struggle reflected in the early fiction.

This conflict of the scientific against the literary attitudes in Wells' own mind was a war of many battles, yet the outcome is foreshadowed as early as *The Time Machine*. In the unfinished early versions, he is writing almost entirely as the literary intellectual, with Hawthorne as his model.[25] The scientist in this version, Nebogipfel, is a kind of demon; the science is a sinister black magic, used neither to do practical good nor to increase pure knowledge. The Time Traveller in the final version is diametrically different: affable and humane. He is disposed to aid the human-like Eloi, and he uses his wonderful machine to obtain new knowledge.

"The Cone"[26] is another surviving fragment which shows an earlier stage of Wells' mental evolution. Horrocks, the ironmaster, is the image of scientific technology. Lacking poetry and imagination, he admires machinery, finding beauty in his blast furnaces, "full of an incessant turmoil of flames and seething molton iron."[27] The adulterer, Raut, is the literary and aesthetic intellectual. Horrocks wins the struggle between them, but only through a symbolic act of self-destructive violence. The story suggests that Wells was torn by the same conflict, and that at this early period he had found no solution that would not destroy his own self-identity.

Though Wells did change sides on this unanswerable philosophic question, moving by degrees from the criticism to the fervid promotion of progress, he was more consistent than he seems. Always, as robust egoist, he had longed for liberation from the past. Always, as biologist and artist, he had been keenly aware of the limits and the relativity of progress. In the great science fiction, he wrestled with his doubts. When he had come to terms with them, he emerged as the great champion of the global utopia.

3   The Live Ideas, 1946 —

If we ever do evolve an integrated and humane world utopia along the lines Wells imagined, that creation of future progress will be the most magnificent possible monument to his far-ranging ideas. Until that happens, however, his most impressive achievement may well turn out to be the anti-utopian criticism of progress in his early science fiction.

In general terms, the opening section of this book outlined his claim to recognition as the chief creator of modern science fiction. At this point, his effect on one specific branch of it calls for more attention. As a questioner of the worth of man's reason, a satirist of scientific truty and man-directed progress, Wells followed and imitated Jonathan Swift. A whole school of skeptics has followed him. This somewhat surprising influence has been ably documented by Mark R. Hillegas in *The Future as Night-mare: H. G. Wells and the Anti-Utopians*.

E. M. Forster's frequently reprinted "The Machine Stops" (1909) is an early story that illustrates the complex and ironic nature of Wells' relation to these followers—who are both imitators and attackers. Hillegas reads Forster's story as an explicit response to Wells' *A Modern Utopia*, published only four years earlier.[28] Wells had come to admire machines, as useful and even beautiful; Forster feared and hated them, as destroyers of independence and individuality. Though Forster's humanistic horror of machines had been foreshadowed in Samuel Butler's *Erewhon*, Hillegas shows that nearly all the details of his story come from Wells—from the earlier scientific romances as often as from *A Modern Utopia*. Forster's human bees, for example, packed into their hexagonal underground cells, seem to reflect *The First Men in the Moon*, and the ventilation shaft which leads to the outside world comes from *The Time Machine*—a novel nearly as anti-utopian as Forster's story. It seems oddly ironic that all these attackers of Wells' later and more optimistic utopian visions should draw so heavily for ammunition on the pessimistic elements of his own first work.

Hillegas mentions the anti-utopian elements in Karel Čapek's *R. U. R.* (1921), the play that gave us the symbol of the robot.[29] As other critics have pointed out, the robots are, in a sense, progeny of Wells; their maker, old Russum, seems to have been Capek's version of Wells' Dr. Moreau, and they were made in an island laboratory much like Moreau's. The play is not really an anti-utopia, however. Capek admired Wells, and his object in the play is not to attack the utopian dream, but "to write a comedy, partly of science, partly of truth." The target of the complex comedy is man himself, the victim of no single illusion, but of many contradictory "truths."

One of the finest works of this dystopian school is *We*, by Eugene Zamiatin—the name is also transliterated as Evgenii Zamyatin.[30] This brilliant tragic satire has a special interest as a disillusioned report on a great contemporary experiment in utopian politics. An old revolutionist who had suffered for his activities against the Czars, Zamiatin was in England in 1916-1917 and came to know Wells' work. His little book, *Herbert Wells* (1922), gives Wells credit for inventing an important new literary *genre* in "social-scientific fantasy"—science fiction.[31] Keenly aware of the social criticism in Wells' "mechanical and chemical fairy tales," Zamiatin draws a sharp line between them and utopian fiction, which he typifies as static and usually plotless. He says Wells "uses his social fantasy novels almost exclusively to uncover the defects of the existing social order, not to create a picture of some paradise to come."[32]

In *We*, Zamiatin uses a far future setting and a richly symbolic style to cloak his disappointed criticism of the new Russia socialist state. His dictator, the Well-Doer, reflects the Lenin he knew in reality as well as the Ostrog he had met in Wells' *When the Sleeper Wakes*. His unfortunate utopians are uniformed and numbered; with no privacy, they live behind glass walls, every act regulated by the Hour Tables. The novel has a classic tragic plot. The narrator, a ship-builder like Zamiatin himself, is defeated and broken in a desperate struggle for individual freedom. At the end he is again the passive subject of the absolute state, watching in satisfaction as the girl he loves is tortured, calmly contemplating the sacrifice of his fellow rebels to "the Machine of the Well-doer."

Hillegas traces most of Zamiatin's powerful symbols back to Wells. Most striking is the "image of the super-city," which Wells had elaborated in *When the Sleeper Wakes* and "A Story of the Days to Come." Besides this supercity, which is a metaphor for the total victory of mechanized society over primitive nature and the individual ego, Zamiatin's plot of the lovers in revolt against it also derives from Wells, as do many other bits of setting and action—the structural glass of the city, the numbered uniforms of the citizens, the brain operation to remove fancy and desire for freedom. Zamiatin himself identifies *We* as Wellsian fantasy of the sort that will mirror post-revolutionary Russia, which has "become the most fantastic of modern European countries."

Hillegas places Aldous Huxley's *Brave New World* (1932) and George Orwell's *1984* (1949) in a "second wave" of anti-utopian reaction.[33] These best-known nightmares of the future are heavily indebted to Wells, not only directly but through Zamiatin. Orwell's book can be read, in fact, as a sort of simplified translation of *We*, transposed from the far future almost into our own times. The Well-Doer becomes Orwell's Big Brother; the oppressive sense of the totalitarian society, of cruel power exercised for its own sake, is almost identical; the same lovers are crushed in the end to serve the total social power that has annihilated their egos. As Hillegas shows, however, many items of background and plot must have come straight from Wells, especially from *When the Sleeper Wakes* and "A Story of the Days to Come," which

Orwell had once admired.

Huxley's *Brave New World* is thematically the strongest of all these anti-utopias. Most of them, like Orwell's and Zamiatin's, are nightmare visions of the worst of all possible worlds. Huxley plays a different and more engaging game. His utopian world is the best, ruled by benevolent statesmen and peopled with contented citizens, scientifically bred and conditioned to fit their social places. Incidental social friction is lubricated with soma; we find no actual inclination toward revolt. Yet this ultimate culture of science is so intolerable to the hero, the representative of the liberal tradition, that he hangs himself.

Huxley himself confessed that the novel was begun "as a parody of H. G. Wells' *Men Like Gods*," which gradually got out of hand. As satirist of specialization, he clearly owes much to Wells' *The First Men in the Moon*. Hillegas traces obligations not only to many other works of Wells, but also to Zamiatin's *We* – which Huxley claimed that he had never read.[34]

In convincing detail, Hillegas proceeds to follow this anti-utopian trend through the famous fantasies of C. S. Lewis and down to the contemporary science fiction magazines. In the trilogy, *Out of the Silent Planet* (1938), *Perelandra* (1943), and *That Hideous Strength* (1945), Lewis attacks the Wellsian utopia, not from the disheartened left, as most earlier critics had done, but from the conservative stance of traditional Christianity. As usual, the weapons come largely from the early Wells; much of the opening book stems from *The First Men in the Moon*.

In *Anthem* (1938), Ayn Rand attacks the utopian ideal from a philosophy of individual selfishness and with symbols borrowed largely from Wells through Zamiatin's *We*. Tracing the anti-utopian theme in recent science fiction, Hillegas mentions many stories – including my own "With Folded Hands" (1947) – and selects three as outstanding examples of the evolution of the anti-utopian theme into popular literature. *The Space Merchants* (1953), by Frederik Pohl and C. M. Kornbluth, is a sometimes brilliantly satiric projection of a world society ruled and manipulated by advertisers. *Farenheit 451* (1954), by Ray Bradbury, projects an anti-intellectual dystopia, whose firemen are employed to burn books. *Player Piano* (1952), by Kurt Vonnegut, Jr., satirizes the elite that Wells had trusted to establish and administer utopia, as they are demoralized and replaced by the electronic thinking machine, *Epicac XIV*. Here, Hillegas says, "we have the best of the recent anti-utopias and at the same time the most profoundly anti-Wellsian."[35]

In all this anti-utopian movement, the dominant emotion is fear—fear of man's universe, fear of his social organizations, fear of his own nature. Historically, the increasing panic of these sensitive and often gifted writers must have come partly from the demolition of traditional beliefs by the ideas of such men as Marx and Freud and Einstein, partly from their emotional inability to keep pace with the accelerated social change due to applied technology. The frightened refugees in search of psychological security sometimes return to religion, as Lewis does, sometimes cling to the artifacts of traditional culture, as do the characters in Walter Van Tilburg Clark's classic story "The Portable Phonograph," sometimes return in imagination to the simpler things of childhood or of primitive nature, as Bradbury likes to do. Just as often, as in Huxley's brilliantly cynical *Brave New World*, they find no enduring values at all.

Too commonly, in our days of headlong change, such fears are fueled by the late news bulletins. Yet I like to recall that the question has two sides. Wells turned utopian, with no violent dislocation of character; so did Aldous Huxley.[36] Related as it is to the eternal tension between self and society, the battle of progress can have no final solution. Every potential citizen of every possible utopia is born with selfish needs and social debts that he must somehow harmonize. However eloquent, pure despair is no solution.

The social criticism of the early Wells and all the anti-utopians is no doubt a good thing, but not everything. Like the older Wells, we are still free to balance our fears of a bad society with practical efforts to build a better one. Even in modern science fiction, the anti-utopians have not yet conquered. Isaac Asimov's robots, safely controlled by his Three Laws of Robotics, are loyal friends and helpers of men. Robert A. Heinlein, especially in his fine juvenile novels, projects a broad panorama of future progress, with science solving problems and men advancing into space. Arthur C. Clarke has written memorable utopias; in *The City and the Stars*, his magnificent Platonic version of the supercity endures a billion years. This reassuring stream of confidence in man and his future also flows into contemporary science fiction through Wells, of course, even more obviously than the anti-utopian tide.

Whatever the verdict on progress, Wells remains the great central figure in modern science fiction. The chief inventor of the *genre*, he fixed its form and created many of its finest models. In an ironic position that few of his critics have understood, he is not only the principal target of the anti-utopian attack but also, in his early science fiction, the most resourceful and most influential of all the attackers.

In summary, we might suggest that Wells' early science fiction is an imaginative laboratory in which he is testing the idea of progress—which is sometimes identified with the culture of science in conflict with the culture of tradition, and sometimes with the egoistic self in its perpetual revolt against social constraints. His reagents are the isolated qualities of the human mind: pure fear, pure hatred, pure selfishness, pure ambition, pure intelligence, even pure benevolence. The tests are severe to the point of destruction, yet somehow the idea survives.

Considered in this way, the early science fiction reveals a remarkable consistency beneath the surface contradictions of Wells' whole work. These imaginative tests show progress to be a precarious struggle for survival in the face of external and internal dangers, where "the implacable law of life" has always been "adapt or perish."[37] As he watched time running out, he grew impatient and discouraged; yet the humane concern of the early fiction clearly animates both the desperate optimist of the middle years and the darker pessimist of *The Mind at the End of Its Tether*.

The first of these imaginative tests, *The Time Machine* (1895), shows possible future human advancement limited not only by the nature of the cosmos but by a self-destructive mechanism inherent in itself. The book also reveals the principle of cultural relativity, with its uncomfortable implication that the successful behavior of one age is likely to arouse the moral or aesthetic revulsion of another.

In *The Island of Dr. Moreau* (1896), Wells tests a series of forces as agents of progress. Natural selection fails, in one view of Moreau's search for the limits of plasticity in living matter. So does human reason, in another view. Human benevolence, in the figure of Prendick, fails more disastrously. Seen from yet another angle, the novel is a test of both science and humanism. Science fails in the symbol of Moreau, humanism in the symbol of Prendick.

In *The Invisible Man* (1897), Wells tests other possible sources of progress. Griffin's pure selfishness fails. So does his pure intellect. Griffin is a symbol of science as amoral power, pitted against satirized images of the traditional literary culture. The test shows pure science, uncontrolled by social tradition, to be both destructive and self-destructive.

In *The War of the Worlds* (1898), Wells is again testing ingeniously purified science and humanism. The scientific culture is that of the Martian invaders; the humanists are their terrestial victims. Stripped of humane ethics and emotions, the culture of science is pure horror. The Martians live like vampires on the injected blood of men. The artilleryman, a human symbol of the scientific culture, is shallowly optimistic, absurdly pretentious, and obviously doomed. But the counter symbol, the curate, is no better for belonging to the formal culture of the literary intellect.

In *When the Sleeper Wakes* (1899), Wells tests another scientific culture which he has created by projecting technological and social trends two centuries into the future. Graham, the Sleeper, is another image of the literary intellectual. Ostrog, the ruthless manipulator of power techniques, stands for the culture of science. Though Wells wavers somewhat in the outcome, the test does show that the scientific culture will move steadily away from the ideal values of the traditional intellectual.

Finally, in *The First Men in the Moon* (1901), Wells tests pure intelligence, emotionless and highly specialized, as a source of progress. Cavor is a computing machine, scarcely disguised with his human mannerisms. The world in the moon is the pure scientific culture, ultimately evolved. The Grand Lunar is the ultimate scientific intellectual. The pure scientific culture is pure nightmare.

Taken together, these novels constitute a striking critique of pure reason. They examine a set of symbols in which intellect is detached from emotion and morality: Nebogipfel, Moreau, the Invisible Man, the Martians, Ostrog, Cavor, and the Grand Lunar. The worlds dominated by these symbols are ugly caricatures of the culture of science. The common theme of these stories is that reason, unrestrained by traditional ethics or by humane feelings, can guide progress only in the direction of hell.

When one comes to summing up Wells' achievements, this criticism of the idea of progress demands first place. A pupil of Huxley in the Darwinian school, he sees mankind as another biological species subject to the laws of evolution. He defines progress as successful adaptive change to meet the conditions of survival. He explores the external limits set upon the human future by the nature of the cosmos, and the internal limits set by the nature of man. Aware that adaptation is always relative to environment, he remembers that ethical ideals are often irrelevant to the evolutionary process and sometimes in conflict with evolutionary reality.

As a literary artist, in the fiction written before he had renounced the means of art, he is also admirable. The inner conflicts that vitalize his early writing arise from the universal ambiguities of life, and the symbolism reveals his own struggle to cope with complex and ironic reality. The emotion is genuine, the detail telling, the workmanship sometimes distinguished.

As a humanist, he is sympathetically aware of the divided nature of man, of all the conflicting demands of the self and society. His profound sense of the potential dignity and greatness of mankind is balanced by an equal knowledge of human limitations. Again and again, he points out the gulf between human nature and human aspiration. Enlightened reason brings the same kind of disaster to the world of Mr. Fotheringay and the island of Dr. Moreau.

As a social prophet, Wells is due more honor than he commonly receives. Although "the shape of things to come is still unclear," as Wagar writes,

> Wells' prophetic career is a kind of bridge, a bridge of ideas, between the perspectives of nineteenth-century Western civilization and the coming world society.[38]

At a time when the nuclear technologists have offered humanity he alternatives of unity or extinction, when an exploding world population is infected everywhere with uncriticized ideas of progress, when every graph of human change is curving upward toward an impossible vertical rate, the social prophecies in the early fiction call for a new consideration.

As a writer of science fiction—which involves being scientist and humanist, social prophet and critic of ideas, literary artist and popular romancer—Wells has not been surpassed.

APPENDIX

Bibliography

ALLEN, WALTER. *The English Novel*. New York, 1958.

AMIS, KINGSLEY. *New Maps of Hell: A Survey of Science Fiction*. New York, 1960.

ATHELING, WILLIAM (JAMES BLISH). *The Issue at Hand*. Chicago, 1964.

BAILEY, J. O. *Pilgrims Through Space and Time: Trends and Patterns in Scientific and Utopian Fiction*. New York, 1947.

BAUGH, ALBERT C., ed. *A Literary History of England*. New York, 1948.

BECKER, CARL L. *The Heavenly City of the Eighteenth-Century Philosophers*. New York, 1960.

BERGONZI, BERNARD. *The Early H. G. Wells: A Study of the Scientific Romances*. Manchester, 1961.

_____. "The Publication of *The Time Machine*: 1894-95," *The Review of English Studies, New Series*, XI (1960), 42-51.

BRETNOR, REGINALD. *Modern Science Fiction: Its Meaning and its Future*. New York, 1953.

BROWN, E. K. "Two Formulas for Fiction: Henry James and H. G. Wells," *College English*, VIII (October, 1946), 7-17.

BURY, J. B. *The Idea of Progress: An Inquiry into Origin and Growth*, intro., Charles A. Beard. New York, 1932.

BUTLER, SAMUEL. *Erewhon: or Over the Range*. New York, 1961.

CATE, CURTIS. "The Road to Moscow: Degaulle and the Kremlin," *Atlantic*, CCXII (August, 1963), 65-71.

CONNER, FREDERICK WILLIAM. *Cosmic Optimism: A Study of the Interpretation of Evolution by American Poets from Emerson to Robinson*. Gainesville, Florida, 1949.

DARWIN, CHARLES. *Life and Letters*, ed. Francis Darwin. 2 vols. New York, 1898.

——————. *The Origin of the Species*. New York, 1958.

DAVENPORT, BASIL. *Inquiry into Science Fiction*. New York, 1955.

——————. and others. *The Science Fiction Novel: Imagination and Social Criticism*, Chicago, 1959.

DE CAMP, L. SPRAGUE. *Science-Fiction Handbook*. New York, 1953.

DICKSON, LOVAT. *H. G. Wells: His Turbulent Life and Times*. New York, 1969.

DOUGHTY, F. H. *H. G. Wells: Educationist*. New York, 1926.

EDEL, LEON, and GORDON N. RAY, eds. *Henry James and H. G. Wells: A Record of their Friendship, their Debate on the Art of Fiction, and their Quarrel*. Urbana, Ill., 1958.

ESHBACH, LLOYD ARTHUR, ed. *Of Worlds Beyond: The Science of Science Fiction Writing*. Reading, Penna. 1947.

GETTMANN, ROYAL A. *George Gissing and H. G. Wells: Their Friendship and Correspondence*. Urbana, Ill., 1961.

GISSING, GEORGE. *The Private Papers of Henry Ryecroft*. New York, 1961.

GREEN, ROGER LANCELYN. *Into Other Worlds: Space-Flight in Fiction, from Lucian to Lewis*. New York, 1958.

HALL, EDWARD T. *The Silent Language*. New York, 1963.

HENKIN, LEO H. *Darwinism in the English Novel: 1860-1910: The Impact of Evolution on Victorian Fiction*. New York, 1963.

HILLEGAS, MARK R. "Cosmic Pessimism in H. G. Wells's Scientific Romances," *PMASAL*, XLVI (1960 meeting; pub. 1961), 655-663.

——————. "The Course in Science Fiction: A Hope Deferred," *Extrapolation*, IX, No. 1 (December 1967), pp. 18-21.

——————. *The Future as Nightmare: H. G. Wells and the Anti-Utopians*. New York, 1967.

——————. "Introduction," *A Modern Utopia*, by H. G. Wells. Lincoln, Nebraska, 1967.

HUGHES, DAVID YERKES. *An Edition and a Survey of H. G. Wells' The War of the Worlds*. Doctoral dissertation, The University of Illinois, 1962.

HUXLEY, ALDOUS. *Brave New World*. New York, 1932.

HUXLEY, LEONARD. *Life and Letters of Thomas Henry Huxley*. 2 vols. New York, 1901.

HUXLEY, THOMAS HENRY. *Evolution and Ethics and Other Essays*. New York, 1898.
_____. *Methods and Results*. New York, 1898.
_____. *Science and Christian Tradition*. New York, 1898.
_____. *Science and Education*. New York, 1898.
_____. *Science and Hebrew Tradition*. New York, 1898.

IRVINE, WILLIAM. *Apes, Angels, and Victorians: The Story of Darwin, Huxley, and Evolution*. New York, 1955.

JAMES, HENRY. *The Future of the Novel: Essays on the Art of Fiction*, ed. Leon Edel. New York, 1956.
_____. *Letters of Henry James*. 2 vols. New York, 1920.

KNIGHT, DAMON. *In Search of Wonder: Essays on Modern Science Fiction*. Chicago, 1956.

LEAVIS, F. R. *Two Cultures? The Significance of C.P. Snow*. New York, 1963.
LEGOUIS, EMIL, and LOUIS CAZAMIAN. *A History of English Literature*. New York, 1935.
LEVINE, GEORGE, and OWEN THOMAS, eds. *The Scientist* vs. *the Humanist*. New York, 1963.
LOVEJOY, ARTHUR O. *The Great Chain of Being: A Study of the History of an Idea*. New York, 1960.
_____. *Essays in the History of Ideas*. New York, 1960.
LOVEJOY, ARTHUR O., and GEORGE BOAS. *Primitivism and Related Ideas in Antiquity*. Baltimore, 1935.

MARTINEAU, HARRIET. *The Positive Philosophy of Auguste Comte*, intro., Frederic Harrison. 3 vols. London, 1896.
MOSKOWITZ, SAM. *Explorers of the Infinite: Shapers of Science Fiction*. Cleveland, 1963.
_____. *Science Fiction by Gaslight: A History and Anthology of the Science Fiction in the Popular Magazines, 1891-1911*. Cleveland, 1968.
_____. *Seekers of Tomorrow: Masters of Modern Science Fiction*. Cleveland, 1966.

NICHOLSON, NORMAN. *H. G. Wells*. London, 1957.
NICOLSON, MARJORIE HOPE. *Voyages to the Moon*. New York, 1960.

ORWELL, GEORGE. *Animal Farm*. New York, 1946.
_____. *Nineteen Eighty-four*. New York, 1949.

PFEIFFER, JOHN E. "The Apish Origins of Human Tensions," *Harper's Magazine*, CCXXVII (July, 1963), 55-60.
PHILMUS, ROBERT M. *Into the Unknown: The Evolution of Science Fiction from Francis Godwin to H. G. Wells*. Berkeley, 1970.

SAHLINS, MARSHALL D. "The Origin of Society," *Scientific American*, CCIII (September, 1960), 76-87.
SCHWALBE, DORIS JEANNE. *H. G. Wells and the Superfluous Woman*. Doctoral dissertation, University of Colorado, 1962.
SILVERBERG, ROBERT, ed. *The Mirror of Infinity: A Critic's Anthology of Science Fiction*. New York, 1970.
SNOW, C. P. *Science and Government: The Godkin Lectures at Harvard University, 1960, with a New Appendix*. New York, 1962.
_____. *The Two Cultures and the Scientific Revolution*. New York, 1959.
SPENCER, HERBERT. *Education: Intellectual, Moral, and Physical*. New York, 1896.
_____. *First Principles*. New York, 1898.
STEVENSON, LIONEL. *The English Novel: A Panorama*. Boston, 1960.

TRILLING, LIONEL. "Science, Literature, and Culture: A Comment on the Leavis-Snow Controversy." *Commentary* (June, 1962), pp. 461-477.

WAGAR, W. WARREN. *H. G. Wells and the World State*. New Haven, 1961.
WELLS, H. G. *Anticipations of the Reaction of Mechanical and Scientific Progress upon Human Life and Thought*. New York, 1902.
_____. *Atlantic Edition of the Works of H. G. Wells*. 28 vols. New York, 1924.
_____. *Boon, The Mind of the Race, the Wild Asses of the Devil, and the Last Trump: Being a First Selection from the Literary Remains of George Boon, Appropriate to the Times: Prepared for Publication by Reginald Bliss, with an Ambiguous Introduction by H. G. Wells*. New York, 1915.

_____. *Certain Personal Matters*. London, 1898.

_____. *The Croquet Player*. New York, 1937.

_____. *The Desert Daisy*, intro., Gordon N. Ray. Urbana, Ill., 1957.

_____. *The Discovery of the Future: A Discourse Delivered to The Royal Institution on January 24, 1902*. London, 1902.

_____. *Experiment in Autobiography*. New York, 1934.

_____. *The Fate of Man*. New York, 1939.

_____. *The History of Mr. Polly*. New York, 1909.

_____. *Man Who Could Work Miracles: A Film by H. G. Wells*. New York, 1936.

_____. *Men Like Gods*. London, 1923.

_____. *The Mind at the End of Its Tether and The Happy Turning: A Dream of Life*. New York, 1946.

_____. *A Modern Utopia*. London, 1895.

_____. "The Rediscovery of the Unique," *Fortnightly Review*, L (July, 1891), 106-111.

_____. *The Short Stories of H. G. Wells*. Garden City, New York, 1929.

_____. *Seven Famous Novels of H. G. Wells*. New York, 1934.

_____. *When the Sleeper Wakes*, intro., Hugo Gernsback. New York, (n. d.)

WELLS, H. G., JULIAN S. HUXLEY, and G. P. WELLS. *The Science of Life*. New York, 1934.

WEST, ANTHONY. "The Dark World of H. G. Wells," *Harper's Magazine*, CCXIV (May, 1957), 68-73.

WEST, GEOFFREY. *H. G. Wells*. New York, 1930.

WHITEHEAD, ALFRED NORTH. *Science and the Modern World*. New York, 1948.

WILLIAMSON, JACK. *Science Fiction Comes to College*. Portales, New Mexico, 1971.

_____. "A Study of the Sense of Prophecy in Modern Science Fiction." Unpublished Master's thesis, Eastern New Mexico University, Portales, 1957.

WILSON, HARRIS, ed. *Arnold Bennett and H. G. Wells: A Record of a Personal and a Literary Friendship*. Urbana, Ill., 1960.

ZAMIATIN, EUGENE. *We*, trans. Gregory Zilboorg. New York, 1924.

Note: Ingvald Raknen's *H. G. Wells and his Critics* (Trondheim, 1962) is a comprehensive survey of Wellsian criticism, listing over 500 articles and reviews of Wells' books; Part VI (pp. 337-419) discusses sources of the science fiction. The H. G. Wells Society has published a complete bibliography, mentioned above.

Notes

CHAPTER I

1. *Fortnightly Review*, July 1891.
2. Appendix to *A Modern Utopia*, London, 1905.
3. *The Short Stories of H. G. Wells* (New York, 1929), p. 922; the story first appeared in *The Strand Magazine*, December 1901.
4. Winter 1928, p. 56.
5. *Seven Famous Novels of H. G. Wells* (New York, 1934), pp. vii-viii.
6. New York, 1895, p. 29.
7. New York, 1967.
8. Jack Williamson, *Science Fiction Comes to College* (Portales, New Mexico, 1971); the three novels are *The Time Machine, The War of the Worlds*, and *When the Sleeper Wakes*.
9. *Experiment in Autobiography* (New York, 1934), p. 106.
10. "A Study of the Sense of Prophecy in Modern Science Fiction," Eastern New Mexico University, Portales, New Mexico (unpublished).
11. Bernard Bergonzi, *The Early H. G. Wells: A Study of the Scientific Romances* (Manchester, 1961).
12. W. Warren Wagar, *H. G. Wells and the World State* (New Haven, 1961).
13. C. P. Snow, *The Two Cultures and the Scientific Revolution* (New York, 1959).
14. See Mark Hillegas, "The Course in Science Fiction: A Hope Deferred," *Extrapolation*, IX, No. 1 (December 1967), pp. 18-21.
15. *Explorers of the Infinite: Shapers of Science Fiction* (Cleveland, 1963), *Seekers of Tomorrow: Modern Masters of Science Fiction* (Cleveland, 1966), and *Science Fiction by Gaslight: A History and Anthology of Science Fiction in the Popular Magazines, 1891-1911* (Cleveland, 1968).

CHAPTER II

1. See W. Warren Wagar, *H. G. Wells and the World State* (New Haven, 1961), an important study of Wells' pioneer efforts to promote the coming world society.
2. H. G. Wells, *Experiment in Autobiography* (New York, 1934), pp. 643-702.
3. *Ibid.*, p. 45.
4. In *Mr. Britling Sees it Through* (1916), *God the Invisible King* (1917), *The Soul of a Bishop* (1917), *Joan and Peter* (1918), and *The Undying Fire* (1919).
5. Geoffrey West, *H. G. Wells* (New York, 1930), p. 213.
6. Amy Catherine Wells, introduction by H. G. Wells (New York, 1928).

7. *Short Stories of H. G. Wells* (New York, 1929), pp. 832-843.
8. *Experiment*, pp. 306-311.
9. F. H. Doughty, *H. G. Wells: Educationist* (New York, 1926).
10. London, 1905.
11. Bernard Bergonzi, *The Early H. G. Wells* (Manchester, 1961), pp. 1-8.
12. See below, Ch. VI.
13. Walter Allen, *The English Novel* (New York, 1958), p. 376.
14. Lionel Stevenson, *The English Novel: A Panorama* (Boston, 1960), pp. 434-435.
15. Geoffrey West, pp. 268-270.
16. Albert C. Baugh, ed., *A Literary History of England* (New York, 1948), p. 1558.
17. Urbana, Ill., 1957; introduction by Gordon N. Ray.
18. F. R. Leavis, *Two Cultures: The Significance of C. P. Snow* (New York, 1963), p. 43.
19. *A History of English Literature* (New York, 1935), pp. 1358-59.
20. Quoted by Anthony West, *H. G. Wells*, p. 215.
21. New York, 1963.
22. Henkin, pp. 253-259.
23. *Ibid.*, p. 259.
24. "The Dark World of H. G. Wells," *Harper's Magazine,* CCXIV (May, 1957), 68.
25. *Fortnightly Review*, L (July 1, 1891), 106-111; see below, The Evolution of the Ideas.
26. Anthony West, p. 73.
27. Leon Edel and Gordon N. Ray, eds., *Henry James and H. G. Wells: A Record of their Friendship, their Debate on the Art of Fiction, and their Quarrel* (Urbana, Ill., 1958); Royal A. Gettmann, ed., *George Gissing and H. G. Wells: Their Friendship and Correspondence* (Urbana, 1961); Harris Wilson, ed., *Arnold Bennett and H. G. Wells:*

(27) *A Record of a Personal and a Literary Friendship* (Urbana, 1960); Gordon N. Ray, ed., *Bernard Shaw and H. G. Wells* (in preparation).
28. Its journal is *The Wellsian*, 21 Fawe Park Road, London, S. W. 15, England. The society has published a complete bibliography of Wells' work.
29. Alfred North Whitehead, *Science and the Modern World* (New York, 1948), p. 201.
30. See below, Ch. IV.
31. Baltimore, 1935.
32. *The Idea of Progress: An Inquiry into its Origin and Growth* (New York, 1932), p. 2.
33. See Bury, pp. 50-63.
34. *Ibid.*, pp. 64-77.
35. See Arthur O. Lovejoy, *The Great Chain of Being* (New York, 1960), pp. 255-262.
36. Carl L. Becker, *The Heavenly City of the Eighteenth-Century Philosophers* (New Haven, 1960), p. 155.
37. Quoted by Bury, p. 221.
38. See H. G. Wells, *Anticipations of the Reaction of Mechanical and Scientific Progress upon Human Life and Thought* (New York, 1902), pp. 112-113; cited hereafter as *Anticipations*.
39. See below, Ch. IV.
40. See Bury, pp. 236-237.
41. *Ibid.*, pp. 334-335.
42. See Herbert Spencer, "Preface to the Fourth Edition," *First Principles* (London, 1880).
43. New York, 1958, p. 450.
44. *First Principles* (New York, 1898), p. 407.
45. *Experiment*, p. 159.
46. *Ibid., p. 161.*
47. *Ibid.*, p. 140.
48. *Ibid.*, p. 12.
49. *The New England Mind: The Seventeenth Century* (New York, 1939), p. 18; quoted by Frederick William Conner,

(49) *Cosmic Optimism: A Study of the Interpretation of Evolution by American Poets from Emerson to Robinson* (Gainesville, Florida, 1949), p. 375, note.

50. Conner, *Cosmic Optimism*, p. viii.

51. See *Experiment*, pp. 574-578.

52. *Ibid.*, p. 12.

53. *The Fate of Man* (New York, 1939), p. 247.

54. *Experiment*, p. 562.

55. London, 1902, p. 74.

56. *Discovery of the Future*, p. 77.

57. *Experiment*, pp. 142-143.

58. *Ibid.*, p. 68.

59. Geoffrey West, *H. G. Wells*, p. 212.

60. Bergonzi, *The Early H. G. Wells*, pp. 150-152.

61. *Education: Intellectual, Moral, and Physical* (New York, 1896).

62. The Romanes Lecture, 1893, included in *Evolution and Ethics and Other Essays* (New York, 1898).

63. "The Dark World of H. G. Wells," p. 69.

64. See Mark R. Hillegas, "Cosmic Pessimism in H. G. Wells's Scientific Romances," *Papers of the Michigan Academy of Science, Arts, and Letters* XLVI (1961), 655-673.

65. See above, p. 26.

66. Bergson's *L'evolution creatrice* was not published until 1907; his influence on Wells was probably small.

67. Especially in "The Book of the Machines," Ch. 23-25.

68. *Life and Habit* (1877), *Evolution Old and New* (1879), *Unconscious Memory* (1880), and *Luck or Cunning* (1886).

69. See Henkin, *Darwinism in the English Novel* (New York, 1963), pp. 94-104.

70. Especially in *The Island of Dr. Moreau*; see below, Ch. IV.

71. New York, 1934, p. 1478.

72. See Edward T. Hall, *The Silent Language* (New York, 1963).

73. See below, Ch. IV.

74. Geoffrey West, *H. G. Wells*, p. 106.

75. P. ix.

76. See below, Ch. IV.

77. See below, Ch. IV.

78. See below, Ch. V.

79. *Ibid.*

80. See below, Ch. III.

81. P. 9.

82. P. 10.

83. "Preface," *Seven Famous Novels of H. G. Wells* (New York, 1934), p. vii.

84. *Experiment*, p. 147.

85. *Ibid.*, pp. 410-424.

86. See below, pp. 35-36.

87. See below, Ch. III.

88. See below, Ch. V.

89. *Experiment*, p. 563.

90. *Experiment*, p. 45.

91. See below, Ch. IV.

92. *Experiment*, pp. 106-107.

93. See below, Ch. V.

94. See Anthony West, *passim.*

95. "The Rediscovery of the Unique," p. 108.

96. See Snow, *The Two Cultures and the Scientific Revolution* (New York, 1959), *Science and Government* (New York, 1962), and Leavis, *op. cit.*

97. In "Science and Culture" (1880), reprinted in *Science and Education* (New York, 1898), pp. 134-159.

98. In "Literature and Science" (1882), reprinted in *The Scientist* vs. *The Humanist*, ed. George Levine and Owen Thomas (New York, 1963), pp. 29-37.

99. *Experiment*, pp. 481-493.

100. *The Early H. G. Wells*, p. 5.

101. *Experiment*, p. 43.

102. *Ibid.*, p. 38.

103. *Ibid.*, p. 154.

104. *Ibid.*, p. 66.

105. *H. G. Wells*, p. 24.

106. Geoffrey West, p. 25.
107. *Experiment*, p. 43.
108. *Ibid.*, p. 238.
109. *Ibid.*, p. 45.
110. *Ibid.*, p. 145.
111. *Ibid.*, p. 520.
112. *Ibid.*, p. 411.
113. See *ibid.*, pp. 410-424; *Letters of Henry James* (New York, 1920), II, 503-508; Leon Edel and Gordon N. Ray, *op. cit.*, and Lovat Dickson, *H. G. Wells: His Turbulent Life and Times* (New York, 1969), pp. 232-259.
114. Henry James, *The Future of the Novel: Essays on the Art of Fiction*, ed. Leon Edel (New York, 1956), p. 273.
115. *Boon, the Mind of the Race, the Wild Asses of the Devil, and the Last Trump: Being a First Selection from the Literary Remains of George Boon, Appropriate to the Times: Prepared for Publication by Reginald Bliss, with an Ambiguous Introduction by H. G. Wells* (New York, 1915).
116. *H. G. Wells*, p. 192.
117. See E. K. Brown, "Two Formulas for Fiction: Henry James and H. G. Wells," *College English*, VIII (October, 1946), 7-17; Lovat Dickson is fuller and fairer.
118. Geoffrey West, *H. G. Wells*, p. 192.
119. *Ibid.*, p. 193.
120. *Boon*, p. 109.
121. *Experiment*, p. 53.
122. *Ibid.*, p. 242.
123. *Ibid.*, p. 311.
124. "Rediscovery of the Unique," p. 111.
125. Quoted by Geoffrey West, *H. G. Wells*, p. 116.
126. *Experiment*, p. 551.
127. *Anticipations*, pp. 3-4.
128. *Ibid.*, pp. 3-4n.
129. See Wagar, *H. G. Wells and the World State*, pp. 164-205.
130. *Anticipations*, p. 154.
131. *Ibid.*, pp. 267-268.
132. *Ibid.*, p. 298.
133. Pp. 59-60.
134. *The Discovery of the Future*, p. 88.
135. London, 1904; reprinted in *Seven Famous Novels*.
136. London, 1906; reprinted in *Seven Famous Novels*.
137. *Works* (Atlantic Edition, 1924), V, ix.
138. See Norman Nicholson, *H. G. Wells* (London, 1957), p. 43; also Bergonzi, *The Early H. G. Wells*, p. 121.
139. "The Dark World of H. G. Wells," p. 71.
140. *Experiment*, p. 157.
141. See Geoffrey West, *H. G. Wells*, p. 157.
142. *Experiment*, p. 401.
143. *Ibid.*, p. 400.
144. *H. G. Wells*, p. 40.
145. *Ibid.*, p. 27.
146. See *Experiment*, pp. 350-361.
147. Geoffrey West, *H. G. Wells*, p. 165.
148. See Wagar, p. 81.
149. See *Experiment*, p. 403.

CHAPTER III

1. *H. G. Wells* (London, 1957), pp. 37-38.
2. *Ibid.*, p. 37.
3. *The Discovery of the Future: A Discourse Delivered to the Royal Institution on January 24, 1902* (London, 1902, pp. 86-87.
4. Pp. 312-313.
5. *Anticipations of the Reaction of Mechanical and Scientific Progress upon Human Life and Thought* (New York, 1902).
6. See above, Ch. II, Sec. 4.

7. Anthony West, "The Dark World of H. G. Wells," *Harper's Magazine*, CCXIV (May, 1957), 68.

8. New York, 1934, p. 293.

9. First edition, 1895; included in *Seven Famous Novels by H. G. Wells* (Garden City, New York, 1934).

10. Bernard Bergonzi discusses and compares the texts of the known versions of *The Time Machine* in "The Publication of *The Time Machine* 1894-95," *The Review of English Studies,* New Series, XI (1960), 42-51; he reprints the first version in *The Early H. G. Wells: A Study of the Scientific Romances* (Manchester, 1961), pp. 187-214; the history of *The Time Machine* in Sam Moskowitz's *Explorers of the Infinite* (Cleveland, 1963), is inaccurate.

11. *H. G. Wells* (New York, 1930), pp. 262-264.

12. *Experiment*, pp. 253-254.

13. Bergonzi, *The Early H. G. Wells*, p. 203.

14. *Ibid.*, p. 196.

15. *Atlantic Edition of the Works of H. G. Wells* (New York, 1924), I, xxi.

16. West, p. 68.

17. First published as a serial in 1897, *The War of the Worlds* is included in *Seven Famous Novels*; the theme is foreshadowed in Wells' essay, "The Extinction of Man," *Pall Mall Gazette* (September 23, 1894), reprinted in *Certain Personal Matters* (London, 1898), pp. 172-179; Wells's brother Frank suggested the idea of interplanetary invasion; for a critical text, based upon unpublished matter in the University of Illinois Archive, see David Yerkes Hughes, *An Edition and a Survey of H. G. Wells'* The War of the Worlds

(17) (doctoral dissertation, the University of Illinois, 1962).

18. L. Sprague de Camp, *Science-Fiction Handbook* (New York, 1953), pp. 15-17.

19. Marjorie Hope Nicolson, *Voyages to the Moon* (New York, 1948), pp. 1 f.

20. P. 458; Wells remarks in the preface to the third volume of the Atlantic Edition that the incidents were so vividly imagined "that now when he passes through that country these events recur to him as though they were actual memories."

21. Bergonzi, *The Early H. G. Wells*, p. 123.

22. See *Certain Personal Matters*, pp. 172-179.

23. Quoted by Geoffrey West, *H. G. Wells*, p. 108.

24. In *Anticipations*; see above, pp. 36-39.

25. The article is "The Man of the Year Million," *Pall Mall Budget*, November 16, 1893. See Bergonzi, *The Early H. G. Wells*, pp. 36-38, and Geoffrey West, *H. G. Wells*, p. 105. The article is reprinted in *Certain Personal Matters*, pp. 161-171, under the title, "Of a Book Unwritten."

26. Bergonzi, *The Early H. G. Wells*, p. 77; Harris Wilson, *Arnold Bennett and H. G. Wells: A Record of a Personal and a Literary Friendship* (Urbana, Ill., 1960), p. 59.

27. Garden City, New York, 1929; this collection is cited hereafter as *Short Stories*.

28. New York, 1937.

29. New York *Herald*, April 15, 1906; quoted by Geoffrey West, *H. G. Wells*, p. 118.

30. *Ibid.*, p. 120.

31. Wilson, pp. 45-46.

32. See above, Ch. II, Sec. 4.

33. *Experiment*, p. 341.

34. *Works* (Atlantic Edition), X, x.

35. *Ibid.*, I, xxiii.

36. *The Country of the Blind and Other Stories*, 1911, p. iv; quoted by Bergonzi, *The Early H. G. Wells*, p. 63.
37. "An Experiment in Illustration," *Strand Magazine* (February, 1920); quoted by Geoffrey West, *H. G. Wells*, p. 106.
38. *Certain Personal Matters*, p. 173.
39. *Works* (Atlantic Edition), X, x.
40. *The Strand Magazine* (December, 1903); *Short Stories*, pp. 111-134.
41. *Short Stories*, pp. 895-907.
42. *The Strand Magazine* (December, 1901); *Short Stories*, pp. 908-922.
43. *Ibid.*, pp. 395-409.
44. *Short Stories*, p. 405.
45. *Ibid.*, p. 407.
46. *The Graphic* (Christmas Number, 1897); *Short Stories*, pp. 631-642; reprinted in Robert Silverberg's *The Mirror of Infinity* with an introductory essay of my own.
47. *Short Stories*, p. 638.
48. *Ibid.*, p. 640.
49. *Ibid.*, p. 635.
50. *Ibid.*, p. 642.
51. *The Pall Mall Budget* (March 28, 1895); *Short Stories*, pp. 266-276.
52. *Short Stories*, p. 275.
53. *Ibid.*, pp. 224-232.
54. *Ibid.*, pp. 207-214.
55. *Ibid.*, p. 211.
56. *Ibid.*, p. 214.
57. *New Review* (1897); *Short Stories*, pp. 613-630.
58. *The Strand Magazine* (December, 1905); *Short Stories*, pp. 88-104.
59. *Short Stories*, p. 89.
60. *Ibid.*, p. 93.
61. *Ibid.*, p. 94.
62. *Ibid.*, p. 97.
63. *Ibid.*, p. 104.
64. *The Pall Mall Budget* (August 2, 1894); *Short Stories*, pp. 198-206.
65. *Pearson's Magazine* (August, 1896); *Short Stories*, pp. 369-385.
66. *The Weekly Sun Literary Supplement*, December 6, 1896; *Short Stories*, pp. 410-420.
67. *Short Stories*, pp. 942-958.
68. *Pearson's Magazine* (March, 1903); *Short Stories*, pp. 844-855.

CHAPTER IV

1. Thomas H. Huxley, "Prolegomena," *Evolution and Ethics and Other Essays* (New York, 1898), p. 11.
2. See Ch. II.
3. *Evolution and Ethics*, pp. 51-52.
4. *Ibid.*, p. 52.
5. *Evolution and Ethics*, p. 83.
6. "The Origin of Society," *Scientific American*, CCIII (September, 1960), 77.
7. Sahlins, p. 78.
8. *Ibid.*, p. 86.
9. *Evolution and Ethics*, pp. 195-236.
10. "The Apish Origins of Human Tensions," *Harper's Magazine*, CCXXVII (July, 1963), 55-60.
11. Pfeiffer, p. 58.
12. *Ibid.*, p. 56.
13. *Ibid.*, p. 59.
14. Geoffrey West, *H. G. Wells* (New York, 1930), p. 179.
15. See above, Ch. II, Sec. 4.
16. *Experiment in Autobiography* (New York, 1934), pp. 400-401.
17. New York, 1939, pp. 228-229.
18. *Apes, Angels, and Victorians* (New York, 1955), pp. 301-302.
19. *Science and Christian Tradition* (New York, 1898), pp. 209-262.
20. *Ibid.*, p. 256.
21. *Ibid.*, pp. 256-257.
22. *Evolution and Ethics*, p. 85.
23. *Papers of the Michigan Academy of Science, Arts, and Letters*, XLVI (1961), 656.

24. Written in 1895, simultaneously with *The Wonderful Visit, The Island of Dr. Moreau* was pub-lished in April, 1896; it is included in *Seven Famous Novels of H. G. Wells* (New York, 1934).
25. "Preface," *Seven Famous Novels*, p. vii.
26. "Note," *Seven Famous Novels*, pp. 156-157; the article is "The Limits of Individual Plasticity," *Saturday Review*, January 19, 1895.
27. *Seven Famous Novels*, p. ix.
28. "Preface," *Evolution and Ethics*, p. viii.
29. "Prolegomena," *Evolution and Ethics*, pp. 16-17.
30. *Ibid.*, p. 17.
31. *Ibid.*, pp. 19-20.
32. *Ibid.*, p. 31.
33. Pp. 50-51.
34. Bernard Bergonzi, *The Early H. G. Wells: A Study of the Scientific Romances* (Manchester, 1961), pp. 97-99.
35. *Ibid.*, pp. 100-102.
36. *Experiment*, p. 45.
37. "Preface," *Seven Famous Novels*, p. ix.
38. Quoted by Irvine, p. 301.
39. *Experiment*, p. 161.
40. Leonard Huxley, *Life and Letters of Thomas Henry Huxley* (New York, 1901), p. 466.
41. *Methods and Results* (New York, 1898), p. 7.
42. *Experiment*, p. 162.
43. "The Dark World of H. G. Wells," *Harper's Magazine,* CCXIV (May, 1957), 69.
44. West, p. 69.
45. *Ibid.*, p. 69.
46. See below, pp. 92-94.
47. See "The Rediscovery of the Unique," discussed above, Ch. II, Sec. 4.
48. See below, Sec. 4.
49. West, p. 69.
50. *Experiment*, pp. 457-458.
51. A shorter, serial version of *The Invisible Man* ran in *Pearson's Weekly*, April-November, 1897; the book is included in *Seven Famous Novels*.
52. Bergonzi, *The Early H. G. Wells*, p. 113.
53. *Ibid.*, p. 113.
54. "Preface," *Seven Famous Novels*, p. viii.
55. Harris Wilson, *Arnold Bennett and H. G. Wells: A Record of a Personal and Literary Friendship* (Urbana, Ill., 1960), pp. 34-35.
56. "Preface," *Seven Famous Novels*, p. vii.
57. Bergonzi, *The Early H. G. Wells*, p. 120.
58. *Ibid.*, p. 120.
59. *Ibid.*, p. 121.
60. *Atlantic Edition of the Works of H. G. Wells* (New York, 1924), V, ix; quoted by Bergonzi, p. 121.
61. See above, Ch. III, Sec. 4.
62. *The Pall Mall Budget* (about 1894); *The Short Stories of H. G. Wells* (Garden City, New York, 1929), pp. 246-253.
63. *Short Stories*, pp. 448-459.
64. See below, Ch. VI.
65. *Works* (Atlantic Edition), I, xxii; see *Experiment*, p. 253.
66. *Short Stories*, pp. 295-305.
67. *The Idler* (May, 1896); *Short Stories*, pp. 351-368.
68. *Short Stories*, pp. 438-447.
69. *Phil May's Annual* magazine (1895); *Short Stories*, pp. 338 350.
70. *Short Stories*, pp. 460-472.
71. *Works* (Atlantic Edition), I, xxiii.
72. *The Pall Mall Budget* (June 21, 1894); *Short Stories*, pp. 191-197.
73. *Experiment*, p. 433.
74. *Short Stories*, pp. 386-394.
75. *The Illustrated London News* (June, 1898); *Short Stories*, pp. 792-810.

76. *Man Who Could Work Miracles* (New York, 1936).
77. *Black and White Magazine* (1901); *Short Stories*, pp. 988-1015.
78. See above, Ch. IV, Sec. 1.
79. *The Strand Magazine* (April, 1904); *Short Stories*, pp. 163-188.
80. *Short Stories*, p. 170.
81. *Ibid.*, p. 171.
82. *Ibid.*, p. 165.
83. *Ibid.*, p. 183.
84. *Ibid.*, p. 184.
85. *Ibid.*, p. 188.
86. In 1939, Wells rewrote the story with a happier ending, in which the blind girl escapes with Nuñez and later marries him, but refuses medical aid because she is afraid to see. Published in a limited edition, this revision has been generally ignored. See Sam Moskowitz, *Explorers of the Infinite: Shapers of Science Fiction* (Cleveland, 1963), pp. 135-136.
87. *Daily Chronicle* (1906); *Short Stories*, pp. 140-157.
88. *Short Stories*, pp. 215-218.
89. *Short Stories*, pp. 517-536; see *Experiment*, p. 159.

CHAPTER V

1. *Bookman,* XIII (1897), 17; quoted by Bernard Bergonzi, *The Early H. G. Wells: A Study of the Scientific Romances* (Manchester, 1961), p. 114.
2. Wells, *Experiment in Autobiography* (New York, 1934), p. 163.
3. *Ibid.*, p. 168.
4. *Ibid.*, p. 183.
5. *Ibid.*, p. 187.
6. London, 2 vol., 1893.
7. See above, Ch. II. Sec. 4.
8. *Science and Hebrew Tradition* (New York, 1898), p. 84.
9. *Evolution and Ethics and Other Essays* (New York, 1898), pp. 80-81.
10. See above, Ch. III, Sec. 3.
11. *Evolution and Ethics*, p. 35.
12. *Ibid.*, p. 85.
13. *Ibid.*, p. 75.
14. *Ibid.*, p. 85.
15. Marshal D. Sahlins, "The Origin of Society," *Scientific American*, CCIII (September, 1960), 82; see above, Ch. IV, Sec. 1.
16. See above, Ch. IV, Sec. 1.
17. See above, Ch. IV, Sec. 4.
18. *Evolution and Ethics*, p. 58.
19. Charles de Gaulle, *Le Fil de l'Epee*; quoted by Curtis Cate, "The Road to Moscow: De Gaulle and the Kremlin," *Atlantic*, CCXII (August, 1963), 70.
20. *Storyteller Magazine* (April, 1921); reprinted in *The Short Stories of H. G. Wells* (Garden City, New York, 1929), pp. 595-609.
21. *Short Stories*, p. 606.
22. *Ibid.*, pp. 923-941.
23. *Ibid.*, pp. 287-294.
24. *Ibid.*, p. 925.
25. New York, 1941, p. 326.
26. *The Pall Mall Budget* (Christmas Number, 1894); *Short Stories*, pp. 254-265.
27. *Short Stories*, pp. 239-245.
28. *Pall Mall Budget* (September 6, 1894); *Short Stories*, pp. 277-286.
29. *Short Stories*, p. 277.
30. *Ibid.*, p. 278.
31. *Ibid.*, pp. 306-314.
32. *Ibid.*, pp. 421-437.
33. *Ibid.*, p. 313.
34. *Strand Magazine* (December, 1903); *Short Stories*, pp. 111-134.
35. *Short Stories*, p. 115.
36. See *Experiment*, pp. 583-584.
37. *Short Stories*, p. 134.
38. *The Idler* (May-September, 1897); *Short Stories*, pp. 643-700.
39. *Pall Mall Gazette* (1897); *Short Stories*, pp. 701-791.

40. Cf. Zit, of Henry Curwen's *Zit and Xoe* (1887), who symbolizes the entire climb from the ape to civilization; see Leo J. Henken, *Darwinism in the English Novel: 1860-1910* (New York, 1963), pp. 174-176.
41. *Short Stories*, p. 644.
42. *Ibid.*, p. 667.
43. *Ibid.*, p. 700.
44. *Ibid.*, p. 702.
45. See above, Ch. III, Sec. 4.
46. *Short Stories*, p. 735.
47. A. L. Morton, *The English Utopia* (1952); quoted by Bergonzi, *The Early H. G. Wells*, p. 151.
48. *Short Stories*, p. 758.
49. *Ibid.*, p. 772.
50. *Ibid.*, p. 773.
51. *Ibid.*, pp. 773-774.
52. *Ibid.*, p. 785.
53. *Experiment*, p. 550.
54. First published 1899; revised as *When the Sleeper Awakes* in 1910.
55. 1906, pp. 11-12; quoted by Bergonzi, *The Early H. G. Wells*, p. 144.
56. *Atlantic Edition of the Works of H. G. Wells* (New York, 1924), II, ix.
57. *Experiment*, p. 494.
58. *Works* (Atlantic Edition), II, x.
59. Harris Wilson, ed., *Arnold Bennett and H. G. Wells: A Record of a Personal and a Literary Friendship* (Urbana, Ill., 1960), p. 44.
60. Royal A. Gettmann, *George Gissing and H. G. Wells: Their Friendship and Correspondence* (Urbana, Ill., 1961), p. 69.
61. *Ibid.*, p. 79.
62. Bergonzi, *The Early H. G. Wells*, p. 140.
63. *Ibid.*, p. 141.
64. See above, p. 38.
65. Bergonzi, *The Early H. G. Wells*, p. 144.
66. "The Dark World of H. G. Wells," *Harper's Magazine*, CCXIV (May, 1957), 70.
67. Bergonzi, *The Early H. G. Wells*, pp. 145-146.
68. *Experiment*, pp. 550-551.
69. See Mark R. Hillegas, *The Future as Nightmare: H. G. Wells and the Anti-Utopians* (New York, 1967), pp. 40-50. and elsewhere, *passim.*
70. Serialized in the *Strand Magazine* in 1901; first published as a book in November, 1901; included in *Seven Famous Novels of H. G. Wells* (New York, 1934).
71. See J. O. Bailey, *Pilgrims Through Space and Time: Trends and Patterns in Scientific and Utopian Fiction* (New York, 1947), pp. 110-112; also Roger Lancelyn Green, *Into Other Worlds: Space-Flight in Fiction, from Lucian to Lewis* (New York, 1958), pp. 138-142
72. *New Maps of Hell* (New York, 1960), p. 40.
73. *H. G. Wells* (London, 1957), p. 29.
74. *Inquiry into Science Fiction* (New York, 1955), p. 6.
75. "Preface," *Seven Famous Novels*, p. ix.
76. *Works* (Atlantic Edition, 1924), VI, ix.
77. See above, Ch. II, Sec. 4.
78. *Ibid.*
79. A scholarly but extremely readable study of the cosmic-voyage theme is Marjorie Hope Nicolson's *Voyages to the Moon* (New York, 1960).
80. *Ibid.*, p. 46.
81. *Ibid.*, p. 77.
82. *Ibid.*, pp. 98-108.
83. See Green, pp. 72-74.
84. Another ship much like that of Wells, propelled in a similar way, is the Steel Globe in Robert Cromie's *A Plunge into Space* (1890); see Green, pp. 114-117.

85. Green, pp. 112-114.
86. Verne's puzzled scorn appears in an interview in *T. P.'s Weekly* (October 9, 1903); quoted by Geoffrey West, *H. G. Wells* (New York, 1930), note, pp. 141-142. "We do not proceed in the same manner. . . . I make use of physics. He invents."
87. "Preface," *Seven Famous Novels*, p. viii.
88. "Prologue," *Science and Christian Tradition* (New York, 1898), pp. 52-53.
89. *Evolution and Ethics*, pp. 24-25.
90. *Ibid.*, p. 26.
91. See "Preface," *Seven Famous Novels*, pp. viii-ix; *Experiment*, p. 106.
92. P. 69.

CHAPTER VI

1. London, 1905, reprinted in facsimile by Bison Books (Lincoln, Nebraska, 1967), with a new introduction by Mark R. Hillegas.
2. *Ibid.*, pp. 7-8.
3. *Ibid.*, p. 98.
4. *Ibid.*, p. 334.
5. *Ibid.*, pp. 165-66.
6. *Ibid.*, p. 265.
7. *Ibid.*, pp. 269-70.
8. *Ibid.*, p. xxxii.
9. *Ibid.*, introduction, p. vi.
10. New Haven, 1961, pp. 208-209.
11. *Ibid.*, p. 275.
12. For a sympathetic recent account, see "The Fabian Battle and its Consequences," in Lovat Dickson's *H. G. Wells: His Turbulent Life and Times* (New York, 1969), pp. 113-133.
13. See Dickson, *passim.*, pp. 134-208.
14. See *The Two Cultures and the Scientific Revolution* (New York, 1959).
15. See Royal A. Gettmann, *George Gissing and H. G. Wells: Their Friendship and Correspondence* (Urbana, Ill., 1961), *passim; Experiment in Autobiography* (New York, 1934), pp. 481-493.
16. Gettmann, pp. 231-233.
17. New York, 1961, pp. 169-170.
18. *Experiment*, pp. 485-486.
19. P. 16.
20. *Experiment*, pp. 306-308.
21. "Science, Literature, and Culture," *Commentary* (June, 1962), pp. 461-477.
22. *The Silent Language* (New York, 1963), p. 37.
23. P. 37.
24. *Ibid.*, p. 170.
25. *Experiment*, p. 254.
26. See above, Ch. IV, Sec. 4.
27. *The Short Stories of H. G. Wells* (Garden City, New York, 1929), p. 452.
28. Mark R. Hillegas, *The Future as Nightmare: H. G. Wells and the Anti-Utopians* (New York, 1967), pp. 82-95.
29. *Ibid.*, pp. 95-99.
30. An English translation of *We* was published in New York in 1924; a Russian version, published in Prague in 1927, raised such a storm that Zamiatin left Russia in 1931, to die in exile. Still banned in Russia, the book is available here as a Dutton paperback.
31. See Hillegas, pp. 99-109.
32. Zamiatin, *Herbert Wells*, p. 141, as quoted by Hillegas.
33. Hillegas, p. 110.
34. *Ibid.*, note, p. 186.
35. *Ibid.*, p. 162.
36. Huxley's late utopia is *Island* (1962).
37. *The Fate of Man* (New York, 1939), p. 247.
38. *H. G. Wells and the World State* (New Haven, 1961), p. 276.

Index:

Works of H. G. Wells

General Index

ONE THOUSAND FIVE HUNDRED COPIES

approximately of this book have been printed and bound by Malloy Lithographing, Inc., Ann Arbor, Michigan, and John Dekker & Sons: Bookbinders, Grand Rapids, Michigan, for The Mirage Press, a non-stock joint partnership, Jack L. Chalker in charge of distribution and Editorial Director, William E. Osten in charge of typography and Production Manager. The type was set on a Varityper direct impression composing machine in 10 and 8 point Century Schoolbook. The paper is an acid-neutralized, archival-quality stock which should not lose either its appearance or strength for many decades of normal use. The books are bound in black novelex, a full cloth binding of exceptional durability.

First printing: February 1973, 1500 copies.
Second printing: September 1974, 1000 copies.